# COMPLETE BOOK OF THE
# HORSE & RIDER

# COMPLETE BOOK OF THE
# HORSE & RIDER

ROBERT OWEN AND JOHN BULLOCK

LONGMEADOW
PRESS

First published in Great Britain by
The Hamlyn Publishing Group Limited
part of Reed International Books

This 1992 edition published by
Longmeadow Press
201 High Ridge Road
Stamford   CT 06904

in association with Reed International Books Limited

ISBN 0-681-41734-X

Printed and Bound in China

0987654321

# Contents

# Introduction

Written for all who are interested in horses and ponies, *The Complete Book of the Horse and Rider* is a valuable additional source of reference to the many excellent books on riding and horsemastership now available. This book makes it clear to the novice owner/rider who wishes to develop his or her knowledge and skill that there is no short cut to success. It emphasises that the primary requirement of those who ride must be to appreciate all that goes into maintaining the well-being of the horse and improving its condition. This should be every horseman's chief concern, and, if done with sympathy and understanding, will bring on an animal to be useful, obedient and contented.

In the following pages the authors, with the aid of effective illustrations, explain some of the principles involved in looking after a horse. In doing so, they lead the reader through the various stages necessary, if success is to be achieved. The opening chapter deals with buying, a subject which to some may appear complex and best left to the more experienced. Buying a horse or pony does demand a certain amount of knowledge, and is important because the process can be costly when mistakes are made. The latter usually occur when the buyer is not certain of the type of horse required or is unclear in his own mind of the purpose for which the horse will be needed.

The book goes on to deal with keeping an animal in a stable or at grass, and looks into the essential requirements to ensure that the horse receives proper care and attention throughout the year. Following chapters discuss common ailments and their treatment, how to clip and the different types of clips, the use of stable rugs, and the grooming routine.

Feeding a horse or pony, an important consideration with regard to an animal's well-being, need not be as involved as many think. There are a number of basic rules for good feeding practice. Once these have been grasped, the responsibility of the owner/rider becomes far more straightforward.

Saddlery and other essential equipment are dealt with in another chapter. The authors look at the selection available, how best to fit and use the various items required for a horse's protection and a rider's control, and how to care for leather and metal fittings.

After explaining the importance of the work of the farrier and illustrating the way shoes are made, fitted and removed, the book moves into the technique of riding, beginning with a comprehensive study of exercising and schooling. Since no two horses or ponies are exactly alike, no hard and fast rules can be laid down concerning the nature or duration of exercise periods. However, this book pays particular attention to the needs of the horse and rider in order to establish an exercising routine and programme aimed at the work being asked of the horse.

Many riders tend to be impatient to compete sometimes long before the correct preparation has been completed. The final chapters describe how to bring a horse forward for competitive riding, covering, for example, the training of a horse for jumping, whether over coloured poles or across country, as well as the demands put on a horse during the various disciplines of horse trials.

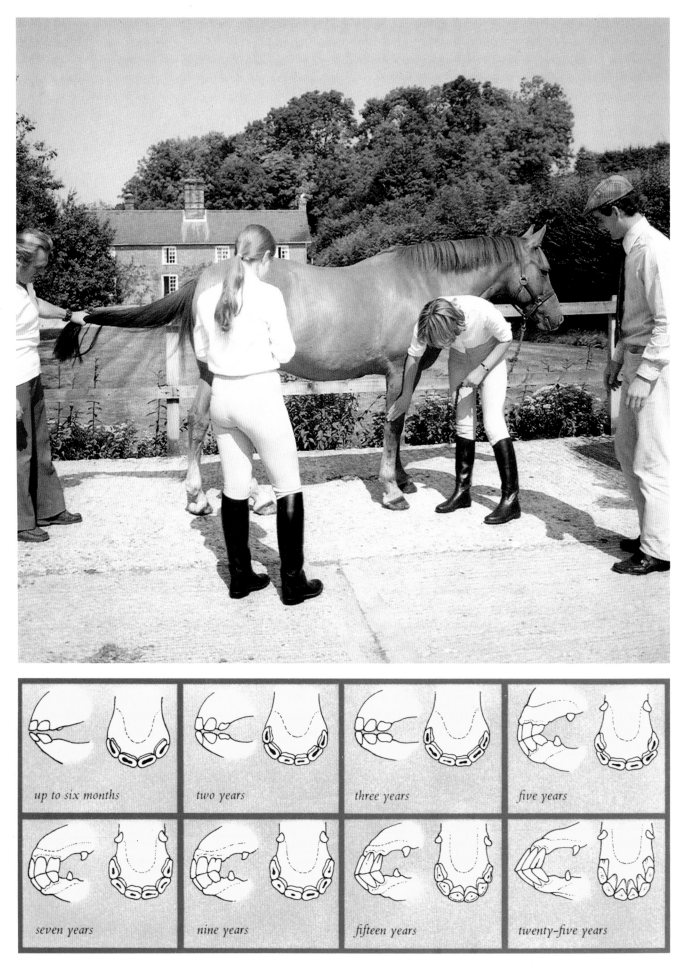

up to six months

two years

three years

five years

seven years

nine years

fifteen years

twenty-five years

# CHAPTER ONE

# Buying a horse or pony

FINDING the right sort of horse or pony calls for considerable thought, patience and care, especially by those with little experience. Having found what is believed to be the right animal there are several aspects to be taken into account, including the animal's soundness, temperament, ability and suitability for the work it will be asked to undertake.

A hasty purchase might prove a disappointment, and in some cases, an embarrassment. Should for any reason a horse or pony fail in one or more of these categories the buyer, on finding he has made a mistake, may not find it easy to sell on. This can bring financial loss, and the search for the right animal, and the cost of searching, will have to begin all over again.

Experience, preferably with the assistance of knowledgeable friends, can minimise risk, but some basic understanding of the horse and how it is 'put together' is to every purchaser's advantage.

In this chapter it is proposed to discuss some of the details which must be borne in mind when setting out to buy.

The first essentials are to have a clear picture of the type of horse or pony required, exactly what he is expected to accomplish, and the maximum price one is prepared to pay. In the case of a pony or a show horse height can also be important, because classes vary according to height.

Native and cross-bred ponies are physically and mentally adapted to living out at grass all the year round, but 'blood' ponies and thoroughbred horses, including Arabians, do not do well if turned out during the winter and need to be stabled, which entails additional work and expense.

*(Opposite, top) If you are sure that the horse you are intending to purchase is the right size, type and price, it should then be checked over for any blemishes or signs of unsoundness, before asking to see it put through its paces. After the animal has passed the preliminary tests as to its suitability, it should be thoroughly vetted by a veterinary surgeon experienced in dealing with horses, who will provide a written report.*

*(Opposite, bottom) The age of a horse is determined by the shape and markings of its teeth, although it becomes increasingly difficult to be certain as to the age of a horse which is over twelve years old.*

The age of the animal is also important. A young horse will need training, whereas one that is too old may not be able to stand up to the work expected of it. If the horse being purchased is a show jumper or a racehorse, details of its career, including its age, will be registered, and the information can be made available to purchasers. Fortunately, however, it is not difficult to tell a horse's age until he reaches the age of twelve after which judging accurately becomes more difficult.

To tell a horse's age it is necessary to look carefully at its teeth. Open its mouth gently by putting a thumb and forefinger on the bar of its lower jaw between the incisor and molar teeth.

A foal's milk teeth begin to appear after about ten days, and take two years to develop into a full set when small dark rings become clearly visible on the biting surfaces. When a horse is three it gets its first permanent teeth, and between three and four distinguishing marks start to appear. By the time it is five it will have grown a full set of permanent teeth, but the corner incisor teeth will meet only at the front. Between the ages of five and seven the incisors gradually meet, and a small hook will appear on the upper corner incisors. At nine years what is known as 'Galvayne's groove' develops on the top corner incisor teeth. This is about $\frac{1}{8}$-inch long to begin with and grows down the tooth. By the age of fifteen the groove will be more than half-way down the incisors, and all the teeth become more triangular and begin to slope outwards. 'Galvayne's groove' will have almost disappeared when a horse reaches the age of twenty-five, but the slope of the incisors will have become very pronounced.

Telling the age of a horse is mainly a matter of practice, and although it is usually extremely difficult to place an animal's age accurately by its general appearance, an experienced judge will be able to notice other tell-tale signs particularly by a horse's legs, and in some instances by its colouring.

Although only certain colours are permissible with some native breeds, an animal's colour is not an indication as to its ability or temperament. It is more important to take careful note of its conformation, which means its build and appearance. A weakness in a horse's conformation can quickly lead to trouble if it is to be asked to perform tasks which place strain, for example, on its joints and tendons.

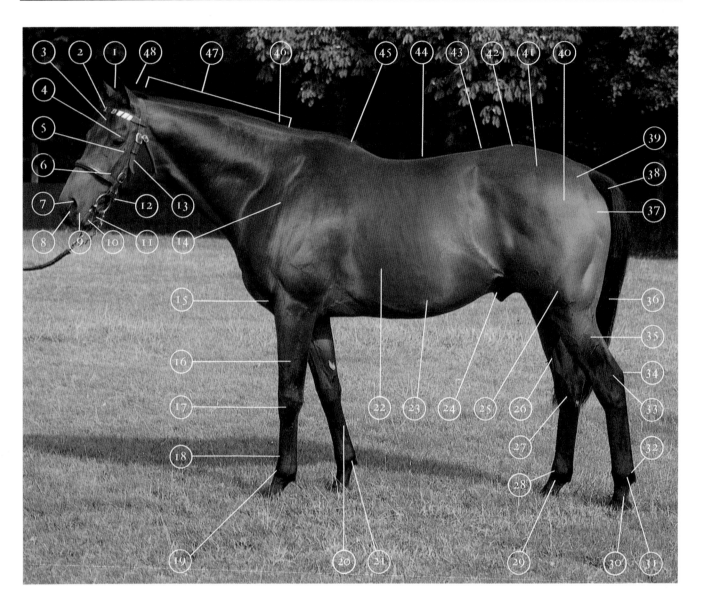

*The points of the horse are shown above on this Thoroughbred. The illustration gives a clear indication of what is to be looked for when considering good conformation.*

| | | |
|---|---|---|
| 1 Ear | 17 Knee | 33 Hock |
| 2 Forelock | 18 Cannon bone | 34 Point of the hock |
| 3 Forehead | 19 Fetlock joint | 35 Gaskin |
| 4 Eye | 20 Tendons | 36 Tail |
| 5 Cheekbone | 21 Ergot | 37 Buttocks |
| 6 Lower jaw | 22 Girth | 38 Dock |
| 7 Nostril | 23 Belly | 39 Hip joint |
| 8 Muzzle | 24 Sheath | 40 Thigh |
| 9 Upper lip | 25 Stifle | 41 Quarter |
| 10 Lower lip | 26 Shin | 42 Croup |
| 11 Chin groove | 27 Chestnut | 43 Point of loins |
| 12 Bars of the jaw | 28 Coronet | 44 Back |
| 13 Cheek | 29 Hoof (wall) | 45 Withers |
| 14 Shoulder | 30 Heel | 46 Mane |
| 15 Pectoral muscle | 31 Hollow of heel | 47 Crest |
| 16 Forearm | 32 Fetlock | 48 Poll |

*(Opposite) A veterinary surgeon checking the action of a horse.*

Although there are many good and genuine horses with Roman noses and lop ears, a horse's head should generally be a good shape and not too big for its neck and body. It should look alert and intelligent and have a good straight neck and strong sloping shoulders. The horse's back should be compact, and it should have a good girth and plenty of chest giving it a good front. Its legs should be clean with good feet which are straight and not at all boxy. The horse should not be 'cow-hocked', with the hocks turned inwards when viewed from the rear.

One aspect of a horse which can be calculated with absolute certainty is its height, which is measured from the ground to the highest point of its withers. The common measurement for horses and ponies is in hands, each hand measuring four inches. If a horse is referred to as being 15.2 hands high it means it measures 15 hands and two inches. Ponies are usually 14.2 hands and below. Above that height they are referred to as horses, except in the case of animals used for polo which are always referred to as ponies and Arabians which, even if they are of pony size, are called horses.

It is important to learn the 'points of the horse', as well as the terms and phrases used for describing different types of animal, so that one is entirely clear as to what the seller means when he describes his horse at the time a decision has to be made whether or not it is worth going to see.

Whatever the type or breed of horse or pony being purchased it is very important to have the animal carefully vetted, and although a trial at home may not always be possible you should try the animal out at the seller's premises, though unfortunately, many bad habits and vices may not show up until some time later.

Having decided on the type, height and age of the horse required it is important to consider the various ways of finding the right animal.

It is safest to buy from someone you know personally. The history of the horse can then be verified and it will be possible to seek the opinions of people who have seen it perform.

Some riding schools buy and sell horses and ponies and, although they obviously must make a profit in their dealings, the reputable establishments, like the more reputable dealers, will go to considerable lengths to guard their good name and to ensure that the animals they are selling are suitable for the work the purchaser requires them to do. They will also often be willing to exchange a horse or pony if it doesn't come up to expectations.

Replying to an advertisement in a local paper or specialised horse magazine is another way of finding the right animal. It may, however, be preferable to advertise for exactly the type of horse required rather than to rely on other people's descriptions. It is then possible to ask for a photograph in addition to details of height, age, experience and price and there is usually less urgency before a decision has to be made to go and see the animal. Those nearest home can be seen first.

Anyone with a limited experience of buying a horse should try to take someone with them who has sufficient knowledge. When going to see a horse ask to have it ridden either by the owner or his representative before personally trying it. If the horse rears, bucks or bolts it is much better to know what to expect before actually buying the animal.

The majority of horses and ponies are, however, sold through sale yards and auctions and the 'warranty' schemes in force at most auctions will safeguard the purchaser to a considerable extent. Even so, the auction ring is no place for anyone without the necessary experience. Seeing horses away from their own stables may mean that bad habits and vices do not become evident until too late.

Even at a sale it is wise to visit a potential purchase in the stable to see how it behaves, though at some auctions, particularly when ponies are being sold, this is not possible because there is insufficient stabling.

Most stable vices result from boredom, and some like rug stripping or kicking the stable door, are not particularly important. Vices such as wind-sucking, when the horse stands with its head raised and neck strangely arched, sucking in and swallowing air with a particular characteristic noise, are far more serious, and horses with that type of vice are best left for other people to deal with.

Crib biting is also a vice often associated with wind-sucking. This occurs when a horse grabs hold of a manger or perhaps the bar of a gate with its teeth at the same time making a strange sucking noise.

Horses who have had the vice for some time can usually be identified because the fronts of the incisor teeth will become worn and look rather like the bevelling on a chisel. Most crib biters will give themselves away, particularly when they are put into a fresh stable, but by then it may be too late to do anything about it.

Crib biting and wind-sucking are frequently the cause of digestive problems, and chronic crib biters will lose condition and be difficult to keep fit.

There is no known cure for crib biting, though one answer is to put the animal in a stable or loose box where there is nothing for its teeth to grab and bite.

Weaving is an even more strange and wearing habit which can be serious. Unlike a crib biter or wind-sucker, an animal who weaves is always likely to pass on the habit to others. A weaver stands at its stable door waving its head from side to side like a pendulum, at the same time moving its weight from one foot to the other.

Providing the vice, for that is what it is, is in its early stages there are one or two courses of action which can be taken. But, unfortunately, no cure is likely. Some owners put a grille over the stable door or have two metal bars

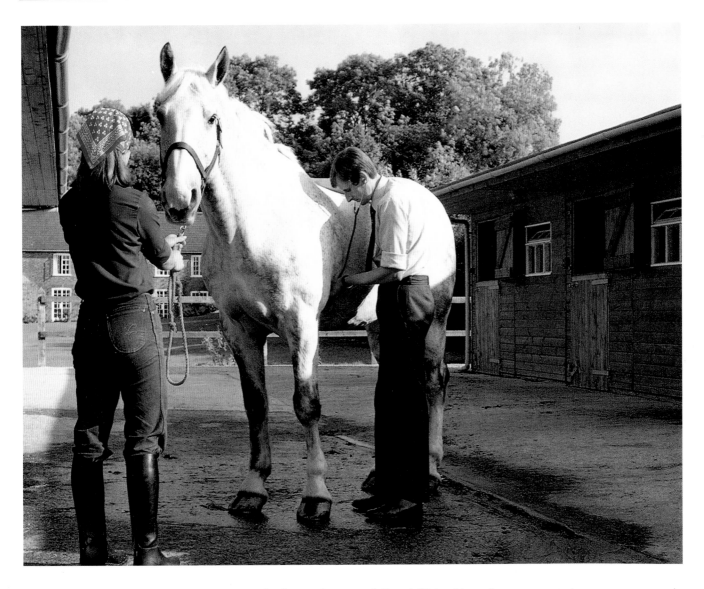

placed in the shape of a 'V' to prevent the horse from weaving when the animal looks out. Another method is to tie bricks to the ends of ropes hanging down above the stable door so that when the horse puts its head over the lower door, and begins to weave, the bricks will strike it on the neck, acting as a deterrent.

Really bad weavers, however, will weave inside their stable, even when the top part of the door has been closed.

Although, as with so many things concerned with horses and ponies, it may sometimes prove difficult to detect vices until the horse has been in the stable for a few days, it is always important to have a thorough veterinary examination carried out before a purchase is made. Following the examination the veterinary surgeon will prepare a written report for the purchaser which details his findings. Should any doubts arise from the report these should be discussed with the veterinary surgeon.

Many vices not attributable to boredom, including biting, napping, bucking, rearing, and all forms of resistance, may not come to light for several months. Some are impossible to eradicate; others may, with patience and careful training, be reduced to manageable levels.

*(Above) Using his stethoscope, a veterinary surgeon examines the heart and lungs of a horse under offer before making his detailed report for the prospective buyer.*

*(Opposite) A type of anti-weaving device which can easily be fitted to a stable door.*

# CHAPTER TWO

# Keeping a horse or pony

ANY HORSE which needs to be fit enough to hunt or to compete successfully will have to be stabled, consequently requiring much more attention than one kept at grass.

It is not just a question of exercise. The stables must be mucked out and kept clean; the horse needs grooming thoroughly each day; it must be fed and its water checked three times or more each day, and in cold weather the horse needs at least a stable rug, and possibly a blanket, in order to keep it warm.

There are various types of stabling. Some are in the form of stalls where the horse has always to be tethered. Loose boxes, which have become much more popular, are larger and enable the horse to be left free so that it usually needs to be tied up only when being groomed, or when it is being saddled and bridled ready to go out.

Whatever the stabling, however, it must be light, airy and draught-proof because horses are susceptible to draughts even though they can often withstand very cold and wet weather when they are in a field. There must also be plenty of headroom and the doors must be wide enough for a horse to get through easily even when saddled. Loose boxes should have doors which are made in two parts to enable the top half to be fastened open to provide ventilation and to allow the occupant to look out. When ponies are stabled a grille is sometimes put across the top part of the doorway when the top half is open to prevent any possibility of the pony jumping out. Ponies in particular can become very clever at getting over the closed lower part of the door, particularly at night when no one is about.

Apart from being wide enough a stable doorway must be at least 2.5 metres (8 ft) in height, and the doors should be fitted with proper stable bolts, with a 'kick catch' at the bottom.

Stables need not be particularly expensive providing they are large enough and do not have any low beams or projections on which a horse can be injured. The walls must also be strong enough to withstand the whole weight of a horse when he gets down to roll.

Stalls are usually about 2 m (6 ft 6 ins) wide and 3.5 m (11 ft 6 ins) long with a 2-metre (6 ft 6 ins) wide passage behind, and a floor which slopes slightly to help the drainage. The horse is tied with its head to the wall usually by means of a strong leather head collar, with a rope or a chain fastened to the back 'D' of the noseband. When a rope is used, the end is passed through a ring usually about chest high and secured by a quick release knot to a wooden ball or 'log'. This method allows the rope limited freedom of movement through the ring so that the horse can move its head up and down, but the rope is prevented from becoming tangled up with the animal's feet.

Loose boxes ideally should have a minimum of about 3 m (10 ft) of headroom with a floor area about 3.5 m (11 ft 6 ins) by 3.5 m (11 ft 6 ins). This amount of space enables a horse to lie down; it is also economical with bedding and easier to keep clean. Horses and ponies can sometimes get into more trouble and mischief in the larger types of loose box probably because they are less careful about the way in which they get up and down and are more inclined to roll over and become stuck against a wall. When this happens it is known as becoming 'cast'.

When a horse is cast, and cannot get up without assistance, it is important to know how to deal with the situation, without hurting either yourself or the horse. Someone is required to sit very gently on the horse's neck near its head to keep it still while you talk soothingly to the animal to try to make it relax. Two pieces of strong rope are then looped around its fetlocks on the legs nearest to the wall. It should be possible to get the horse back on to its feet by giving a gentle, steady pull on the ropes. Care, however, must be taken to ensure that there is a steady pull and not a jerk, or the horse's back may be damaged.

The horse should then be trotted along a level piece of ground to make sure that it moves easily and evenly. If there are any doubts a veterinary surgeon should be asked to check that it has not knocked itself or dislocated any vertebrae in its back.

In both loose boxes and stalls the windows need to be situated high enough to be out of the way of a horse's head. They should be hinged at the bottom so that they will open inwards and preferably have bars or be covered with wire mesh for safety. The glass should be cleaned regularly to allow plenty of light into the box.

Light switches must be of the safety variety and out of reach of the horse. Some animals become very clever at

*(Opposite) An excellent stable block, with four contented horses. The ideal form of ventilation is illustrated – with the upper front windows opening inwards – as is the best type of fittings to secure the stable doors.*

turning lights on unless the switches are out of harms way. The lights must also be well out of reach and protected either by toughened safety glass or by wire cages.

Stables need few fittings. Mangers look attractive but they are usually difficult to clean and, as a horse's natural feeding position is with his head on the ground, a good size bowl with a flat bottom is not only better, but it can also be taken away and cleaned as soon as the feed is finished. In addition there is less likelihood of any of the food becoming stale.

Horses bedded down on straw will require a tie ring for the hay net. This should be placed in the wall high enough to keep the net away from the animal's feet when the net becomes empty, but low enough to prevent hay seeds from getting into its eyes.

A strong ring for tying up a horse when it is being groomed or saddled is also required. It should be fixed level with a horse's breast, preferably having a loop of string or twine tied to it. The rope attached to the head collar is then tied through this loop, and not through the

*(Opposite, top) A fork is being used to make a bed from wood shavings. Particular attention must be paid to ensure that the shavings are packed high against the corners formed by the walls and floor of the stable, and that there is a good thick layer of shavings.*

*(Opposite, bottom) A 'tack' room showing neatly hung bridles and saddles. For many, the neatness of the tack room is a sign of the efficiency and organisation of the stable yard.*

*(Left) Hay must be kept undercover, preferably in an open barn where air can circulate.*

*(Below) Another view of the 'tack' room, clean and well organised and equipped with sufficient saddle racks.*

ring. Should a horse suddenly move backwards the string or twine loop will break and the head collar will not be damaged.

Some stables are equipped with automatic water bowls. These can save time and effort and will ensure a constant supply of fresh water. The snag to using automatic water bowls is that it is never possible to know how much water an animal has taken. One or two plastic water buckets, or a small plastic dustbin placed in a corner of the stable can be more satisfactory. It then is easier to tell whether, for any reason, a horse is not drinking the quantity it should.

The buckets, however, should be checked at least three times a day, and are best placed near the door of the stable where they are easier to see and re-fill. Every morning they must be emptied, cleaned and re-filled, and at least once a week they must be thoroughly scrubbed.

It is essential for horses to have a constant supply of fresh water. In their natural state, where they may have a stream running through their field, water is always available

*(Above and left) How to make a quick release knot – useful when tying up a horse.*

*Illustrated opposite are some of the plants, shrubs and trees which can be dangerous to horses and ponies when eaten in excess: 1 Kidney vetch; 2 Ragwort; 3 Hemlock; 4 Privet; 5 Foxglove; 6 Horsetail; 7 Rhododendron; 8 Ground ivy; 9 Conifer; 10 Oak (acorns); 11 Yew; 12 Bracken (when growing).*

during much of the year. It is when they are kept from water that horses sometimes drink larger quantities at one time than is good for them. Remember that a horse is less likely to get colic when a continuous supply of fresh water is available.

The ideal floor of a stable is one made from concrete with a slight slope to assist drainage, but other bases are suitable providing the floor is dry and can be kept clean.

The kind of bedding used must depend on various considerations. Straw, as now produced, is, unfortunately, often dusty and can be the cause of coughing. Indeed, some horses and ponies are allergic to straw and have to be bedded down on other forms of bedding.

If wheat straw is used, which is preferable to barley or oat straw, it should be dry, free from mould and dust, and light grey in colour. Straw that has become dark and almost black is to be avoided.

Wood shavings can sometimes be dusty and have to be watched, but they do make a good form of bedding. Other materials which may be used efficiently include sawdust, peat moss, dried bracken and shredded paper.

The eventual choice will probably depend on availability and cost, and whether or not the horse is allergic to straw. All beds have to be re-made each day and the stable 'mucked out'. The equipment needed will include a good-sized wheelbarrow, a shovel, a brisk broom and a skip. Beds, where wood shavings have been used, will require the use of a rake. To handle straw a long-pronged fork is desirable. But, it is strongly recommended that thick rubber gloves are worn; there is much the hands can do, and do more easily!

A harness room, or tack room as it is usually called, must be equipped with sufficient saddle racks, bridle cups or hooks and a saddle horse on which to clean saddles. A large vermin-proof box or container, in which to store un-used rugs and blankets and other items of saddlery not in use, will prove valuable. A cupboard to store bandages, cleaning materials and smaller miscellaneous items will be found useful. The medicine cabinet should be fixed to a wall and be easily accessible.

The food store, which ideally should have a supply of fresh water nearby, will require vermin-proof containers in which to store bran and oats and other foods of that nature. Large plastic dustbins with lids can be satisfactory. With feed being so expensive it is important to prevent waste, either through the food becoming contaminated or damp. Vermin will quickly detect any food left lying around or open to them – everything must be done to keep vermin away from the stable complex.

Hay and straw are best kept in a specially constructed barn or store room.

The old saying 'a place for everything and everything in its place' is sound advice as far as stable management is concerned, but to 'everything in its place' should be added 'with cleanliness and tidiness'.

## AT GRASS

Although grazing is the natural way for horses to eat, they cannot be turned loose into a field and left to fend for themselves. They need daily attention if only to make sure there is a supply of fresh and clean water.

In winter months they will require supplements of hay as well as regular feeds of concentrates like pony nuts and bran. In the case of horses and ponies not in steady work feeding oats may make them too fresh.

Horses at grass have little opportunity of finding nutritious food when the grazing is poor, and the condition of the land needs watching. Once land is in a run-down state it becomes much more difficult to keep up the quality of grazing.

In the wild, horses and ponies are able to forage and look for food, sometimes travelling many miles each day in order to find enough to eat so the pasture does not become stale. However, life for these animals, especially in hard weather, is tough indeed, and survival more difficult.

During the months of spring and early summer the problem is reversed. Grass becomes rich and lush, and horses and ponies become fat and vulnerable to various diseases caused by overeating. The most common disease at such times is laminitis, or 'fever of the feet', an inflammation of the sensitive tissues which line the inside wall of the foot. Laminitis can also arise from too much fast work on hard ground and from insufficient exercise.

An animal with laminitis will be in acute pain, reluctant to move, and will try to stand with all its weight on its heels. In bad cases ridges form round the feet. Horses and ponies with laminitis must have immediate attention and treatment from a veterinary surgeon.

When the grass is rich grazing should be reduced to a few hours each day. If possible, it is sensible to keep horses and ponies in their stables during the day and turned out at night when there are fewer flies.

Growing in most fields and paddocks is a variety of common weeds. These require cutting down and destroying at frequent intervals. But, common weeds must not be confused with poisonous trees and plants which are dangerous to horses and ponies when eaten in excess. Some of these are illustrated on page 19.

Of all the trees and plants which must be kept out of the reach of horses particular mention must be made of ragwort. Where this is found it should be dug up and burned.

*(Opposite, top) The best type of water trough is one with its supply controlled by a stop-cock and valve, which will ensure fresh, clean water at all times.*

*(Opposite, bottom) Post-and-rail fencing is one of the best ways to divide fields or paddocks. This illustration shows the use made of post-and-rail fencing. In the foreground is a tidy muck heap of shavings which can be burnt or left to rot.*

Ragwort is dangerous at all times, even when dead, and it never helps to pull the plant from the roots and leave this lying on the ground.

Most horses will ignore ragwort, providing there is good grass. But there is always the risk that this plant will be eaten, producing liver damage which may not become apparent for several weeks after it has been taken into the digestive system.

Another great problem arises from fields which are neglected in that they have become 'horse sick'. Fields which are 'horse sick' will be identified by their patchy appearance. Patchiness will also arise where horse droppings are left and not picked up and removed to the muck heap, but in this case the grass will grow in long tufts which horses will not eat.

Three, sometimes four, times each year horses and ponies will require worming, to rid them of the worms which breed quickly and profusely in their intestines, and when that happens large quantities of eggs are passed out with the droppings which contaminate the land.

A large field should be divided in half, with one half being rested and treated while the other half is being grazed. Professional advice should be sought where there are signs of 'horse sick' or sour land. Chain harrowing and rolling helps to improve such land, but much more has to be done to it than this if land is to be brought back to good condition.

Effective drainage can play an important role in the quality of grazing. There are many different types of soil and subsoil, making the questions of drainage much more complex. Two totally different types of soil can be found in one field, and the main problem is to prevent excess water lying for too long. Many fields become extremely wet and boggy during winter months, increasing the possibilities of mud fever.

The ground near water troughs and gateways, and places used for supplementary feeding, quickly become cut up. That is a problem in itself during winter months; it is compounded during the summer when these areas become hard and cracked!

Fields of all types require proper fencing or close hedging. And this must be inspected regularly throughout the year. A good, safe fence is important not only for the safety of the horses and ponies being grazed, but will also prevent animals from destroying or damaging other people's property.

A post-and-rail fence, built to a height of approximately 1.4 m (4 ft 6 ins) is best, although hedges, when free from poisonous trees and plants, and providing there are no gaps, can be very effective. A constant supply of clean, fresh water is essential, as well as a field shelter.

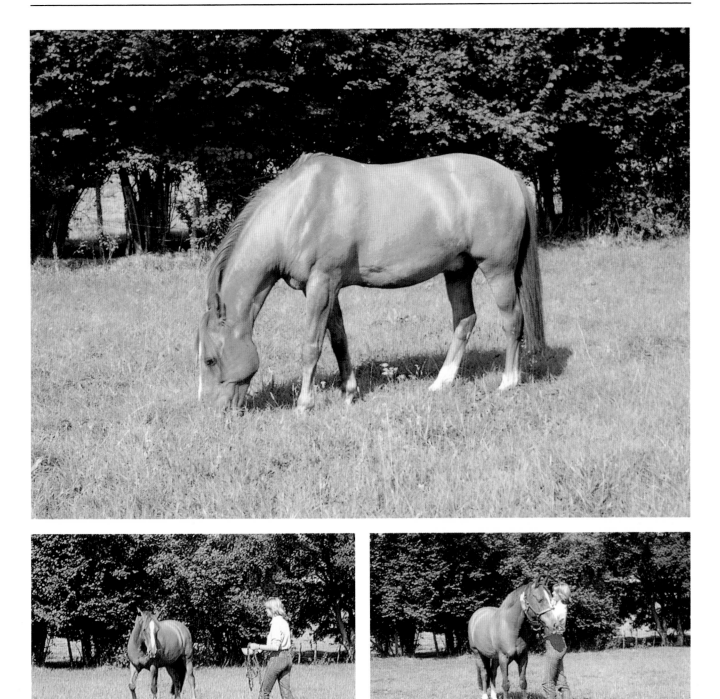

*A sequence of illustrations showing the correct way to catch a horse: (Top) The horse is quietly grazing and does not appear to be disturbed by the person approaching. (Above, left) With a bowl of nuts or a suitable tit-bit the person approaches the horse from the front encouraging it to come forward, while quietly talking to it. (Above, right) Having rewarded the horse with some of the nuts the head collar is placed gently over the horse's head. (Left) The horse is now ready to be led from the field, knowing that it will be given the remainder of the nuts on reaching the stable. This will encourage it to be caught next time.*

*(Opposite) Owners should frequently check the condition of fencing and hedgerows. Here is a clear example of badly maintained fencing.*

23

A shelter should be built with its back against prevailing winds and have an opening wide enough to allow horses to move in and out quite freely. It must be constructed in a solid fashion since it will have to withstand the wear caused by the animals rubbing.

The suggestion that horses lie down to sleep more in the winter than in the summer is not true. In the winter they walk about at night to keep warm, and usually lie down during the day when it is warmer. During the summer months, however, they may lie down for a few hours during the night or early in the morning when not many people are about to see them; this may account for the belief that horses sleep more in winter.

The most concentrated eating periods for horses at grass are just after dawn and before dusk. They seldom graze when it is really dark, and it is for this reason that they frequently break out of their fields at night rather than during daylight hours. They wander about, trying to keep warm, and, with nothing to do, are more likely to find any unmended gap in a hedge or fence.

After a horse has had its early morning graze it will often spend time picking at pieces of grass rather than continuing to graze normally. It is this tendency to 'pick' at bits of

*(Above) An illustration showing a mobile stable which has been developed and patented by one of the leading makers of horse-boxes. The value and use of the mobile stable is given on page 26.*

*(Opposite) A head collar must always fit correctly and be kept in a clean and well-maintained condition. This leather head collar is fully adjustable to fit various sizes of horse.*

grass that has also led to the suggestion that horses and ponies are bad grazers.

Before any animal is turned out it is important for someone to go over the ground carefully to make sure that there are no pieces of wire or broken bottles which might cause injury.

Horses, fortunately, are generally sensible animals who manage to cope with holes and areas of rough ground quite satisfactorily, providing they are not forced to gallop too fast over them. They can, however, be hurt by treading on wire or broken glass which may lie hidden. It is much better to be safe than sorry, and a few minutes spent going over a field carefully can save considerable trouble later, quite apart from preventing the suffering which may be inflicted on the horses.

# THE MOBILE STABLE

Mobile stables, which can be towed behind a large car or horsebox, are becoming extremely popular, particularly among competitors who travel long distances with their horses, and who do not want their horses stabled in poor quality stables, or where they may come into contact with some contagious disease.

The mobile stable folds up into a trailer for travelling and can be opened up on arrival to form one or two loose boxes or up to six stalls. When not in use it can be stored in a corner of the yard.

Some owners also use this type of stable at home as additional stabling or as isolation boxes, because they can be erected some distance from the stable block. They are also useful to parents who turn out their children's horses or ponies during term time but need stabling during school holidays.

# COMMON AILMENTS AND THEIR TREATMENT

Good stable management is the best precaution against illness. There is no satisfactory substitute for careful feeding; regular, sensible exercise; and expert shoeing. Unfortunately, even horses which are well looked after can pick up a virus or get injured, and when that happens the wisest course of action is usually to seek good professional advice.

A horse which does not get the correct treatment quickly will be out of action longer, and the final cost will no doubt be higher. There are, however, some common illnesses which should be easy to recognise, and which will respond to treatment quite quickly, providing the person looking after the horse can diagnose what is wrong, and knows the correct action to take.

Bad feeding can be avoided but it is still the cause of many of the most common forms of illness in horses and ponies. Colic is a term caused to describe any type of pain in the stomach which can range from a mild attack of indigestion to a serious stoppage in the bowels, or even a twisted gut which may require surgery, and can even prove fatal. The first indication that something is wrong occurs when the horse shows obvious signs of discomfort, and starts lying down and getting up at frequent intervals, swishing his tail and looking round at his flanks. It may lie flat for a while and then start to roll. The horse will also probably try to stale or pass dung.

It is unfortunate that the early stages of colic rarely give a clear indication of the seriousness of the attack. This means that all signs of colic must be dealt with swiftly, and a veterinary surgeon should be called if the horse starts to show any signs of real distress or if the pulse rate increases to more than 80 or 90 beats a minute. The normal pulse rate is between 36 and 40 beats a minute, which can be checked by putting a finger on the submaxillary artery at the point where it passes under the jawbone. In severe cases of colic a horse may become violent and throw itself about its box in its efforts to try and relieve the pain.

Sometimes the horse will go down on its hind-legs and try to crouch, rather in the same way as a dog will sit, but in the case of a horse it is a bad sign. The membrane of the eyes may also turn from pink to a dark colour.

The various old and modern types of colic drenches may relieve the symptoms, but they will not always cure the problems. It is far wiser to call the veterinary surgeon and while awaiting his arrival try to keep the horse as warm as possible by putting on extra blankets, and then walk it slowly to prevent it from lying down or trying to kick out at its stomach.

Horses get indigestion far more frequently than many owners realise. Sometimes the problem is worms, but more often the cause can be a badly balanced diet, musty food, irregular feeding, insufficient exercise, allowing the horse to bolt large feeds when it is tired, or allowing it to drink large quantities of very cold water when it is hot and sweating.

A stoppage of the bowels may be due to an animal eating musty or heated hay or decaying weeds, and the condition can be dangerous if the veterinary surgeon is unable to reach the obstruction and remove it. Fortunately a twisted gut is relatively unusual. It can be caused by a heavy fall when the intestines are full of food and the horse is being ridden too soon after a large meal, or because it has been given too strong a purge following a stoppage in the bowels. Unfortunately, a twisted gut is usually fatal, because although revolutionary progress has been made with horses in bone surgery, internal surgery still presents a real problem.

Many problems relating to a horse's digestion and general well-being are caused by worms, and that is why they must be wormed regularly and given the correct dosage. There are several varieties of red worms and the intestines of a horse provides a natural breeding ground. When worms live in the intestines they not only take much of the nourishment from the food, but also stick to the intestine walls where they suck the blood and cause anaemia. Horses with worms lose condition, and their coats have a dull and harsh appearance. Seat worms are not so injurious to health but they are a nuisance, and may cause horses to rub their tails.

Horses and ponies out at grass frequently suffer from bots in the summer. Although bots are not strictly worms they are parasites which live inside the stomach and they too may need removing with one of the anti-worm preparations.

The bot is really a pupa which matures in the spring and detaches itself from the lining of the stomach to pass out with the droppings. Soon afterwards it develops into a large fly rather like a hornet but without a sting. The female lays eggs on the horse's coat, usually in the region of the legs, which can be seen quite clearly on horses at grass. The horse then licks the eggs transferring them into the stomach and so the process continues. There are various methods of dealing with the eggs when they are on the

*(Below) The veterinary surgeon is watching closely the performance and behaviour of this horse for any signs of malfunction in its breathing. After the horse has done some strenuous work the vet will also be able to use a stethoscope to check the heart and lungs.*

*(Bottom) Illustrated is the exercise bandage (group on left), which must always be put on over cotton wool or gamgee, and the travelling bandage (group on right), which may also be used with gamgee or on their own.*

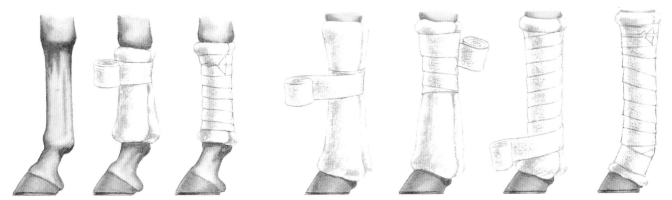

*(Right) A hoof showing severe sandcracks.*

*(Below) Horses are unable to chew their food satisfactorily when their teeth become sharp. Therefore, their digestion can be affected. When that happens the teeth must be rasped smooth by a veterinary surgeon. As the picture shows, the rasping should not cause any undue discomfort, when it is done correctly.*

*(Opposite) A wise rider will check the tendons of a horse after it has returned from exercise or strenuous work. If the tendons show any signs of being puffy or sore, or if there is any heat present in the legs, immediate attention will be necessary.*

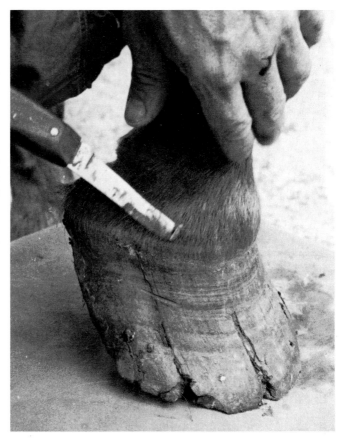

horse's coat, but probably the most effective is to shave them off very carefully with a safety razor.

Apart from skin diseases, which have been dealt with in another chapter, and digestive ailments, horses are also very susceptible to colds, coughs and influenza. The treatments can vary according to the cause, but on no account should a horse be worked if it has a temperature or any unusual discharge from its nose. Some horses, like some people, always seem to have a slightly runny nose, but a cough and runny nose together should on every occasion be treated seriously.

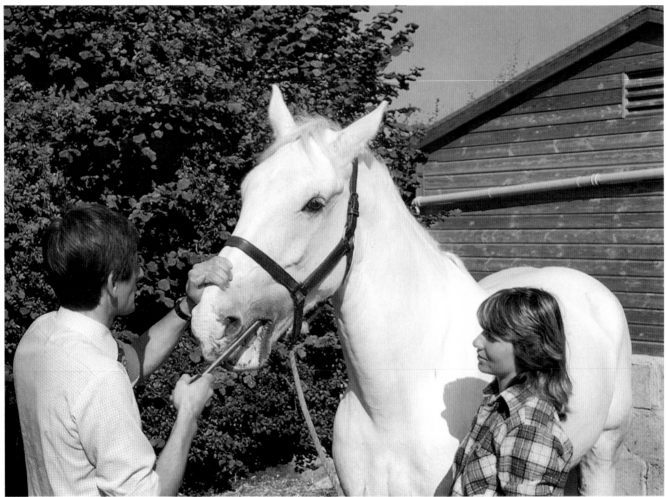

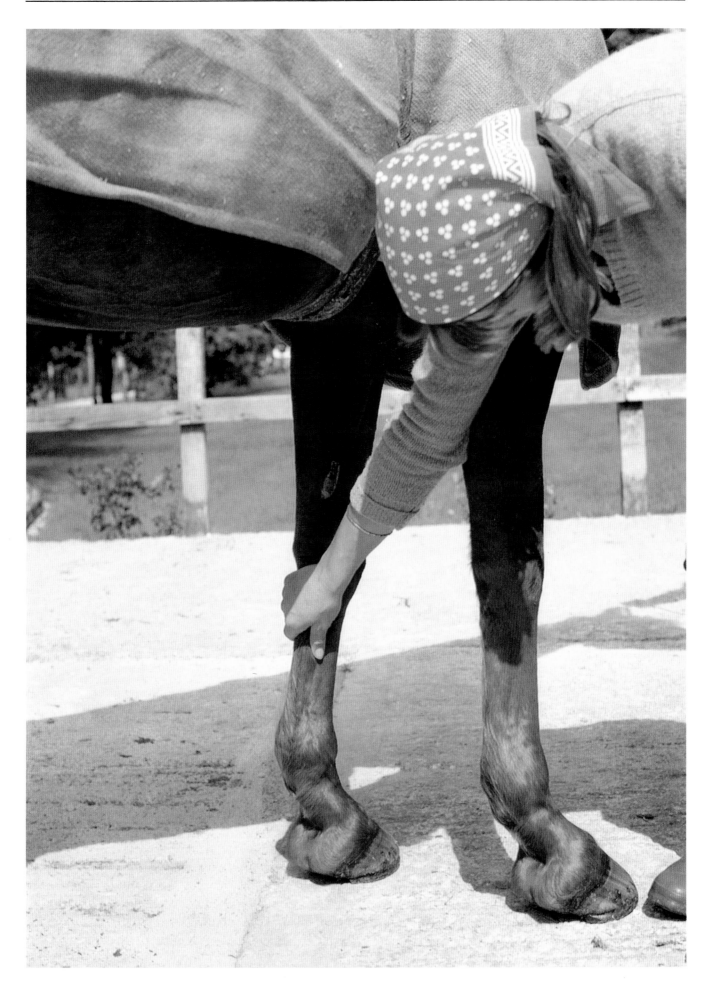

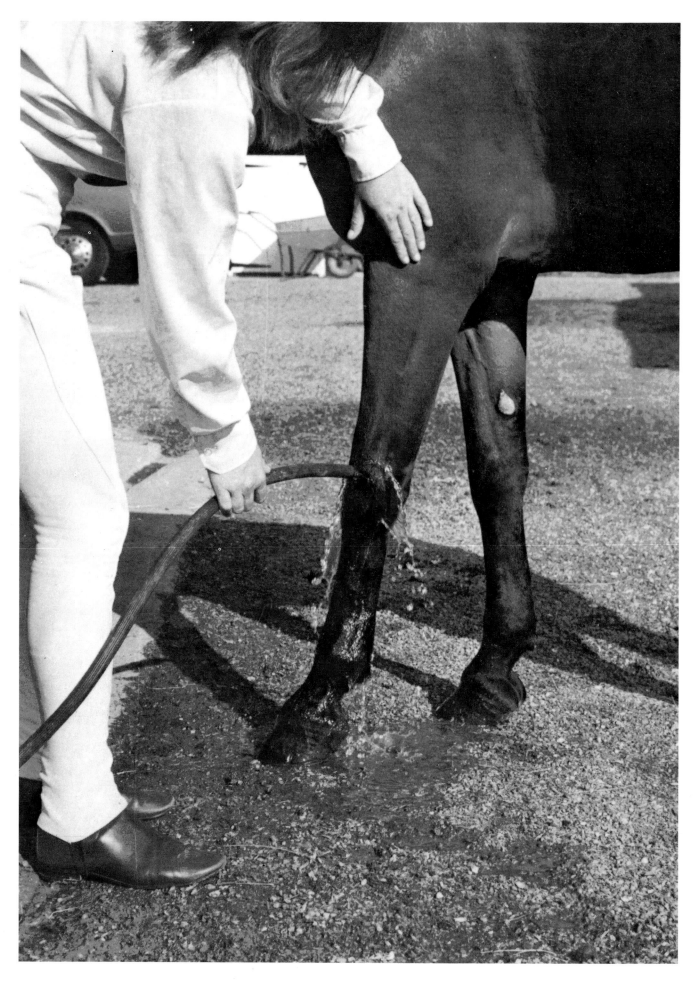

*(Opposite) Cold water, applied through a hosepipe, helps to remove or reduce heat from a horse's leg. The water must always be applied in the form of a steady trickle – never allow the pressure to get too high.*

'Broken wind' is a term covering various chronic lung conditions. If it is caused by an allergy its effects can be alleviated by finding out the cause of the allergy. It may be dust from poor quality straw, in which case shavings or some other form of bedding should be used, because the horse may be allergic to straw.

The symptoms of broken wind are a deep persistent cough, and a horse's flanks can be seen to heave twice during breathing out. Horses affected by dust should be given hay and other feeds which have been dampened, and in really bad cases hay substitute cubes may be needed.

Whistling, which can be hereditary, only occurs in the larger type of horse. It usually makes a high-pitched noise when breathing in, rather like a whistle, particularly during fast work. It is a condition that follows paralysis of one of the nerves of the larynx, and which may be helped by a Hobday operation.

A condition which used to be very prevalent among driving horses who worked hard all week but were still fed the same amount of food on their Sunday off, is known as 'Monday sickness', or Azoturia, to give it its medical term. The symptoms are cramp in the muscles of the loins and quarters which may cause a horse to move only with great difficulty. The horse will sweat and run a temperature, and its breathing rate will probably be rather quick.

If the attack occurs away from the horse's stables, transport will be needed because it will be unable to walk very far. It must be kept warm and given plenty of water which has had the chill taken off it, along with a bran mash with a liberal helping of salt. If possible gentle heat should be applied to the affected areas, and the veterinary surgeon will probably give the horse an injection to relax the muscles. The condition should be treated seriously, and because it can recur, particular care must be taken over the diet and exercise of any horse which has had the complaint. In order to prevent illnesses like Azoturia, horses need to be given less food when they are off work and should be fed bran mashes.

Many leg and foot problems could also be avoided with a little more care. Thrush, for example, is a disease of the foot usually caused because the feet have not been picked out properly, or the bedding has been allowed to get too dirty and damp. There will be a nasty smelling discharge from the frog which needs to be cleaned with soap and water, and when dry Stockholm tar should be applied to the affected area.

Lameness can also be caused by corns, which in the case of horses are really bruises which occur in the foot near the heel, between the frog and the wall. The trouble can usually be cured by removing the shoe and cutting away the horn in the affected area until the discoloration of the bruise appears. Some horses seem to suffer from corns far more than others.

Sandcracks may appear when there is a split in the wall of a hoof which has become too brittle. A skilled blacksmith can prevent the crack from opening any further, and the horn can be encouraged to grow by the application of a mild blister to the coronet band.

A much more serious disorder, however, is laminitis, which is sometimes referred to as 'fever of the feet', because there is inflammation of the sensitive tissues lining the inside wall of the foot. Laminitis is caused by too much lush grass or rich food without adequate exercise. The shoes must again be removed and the feet cut down and hosed frequently with cold water. Great care will have to be paid to diet and the veterinary surgeon will also probably give a pain-killing injection.

Navicular disease affects the navicular bones of the front feet, and is caused by thrombosis in the local blood vessels. The trouble may be hereditary and brought on by too much work when the ground is very hard. The disease has previously been considered incurable, but new treatments are now being tried with encouraging success.

Splints usually occur in a young horse either as a result of a blow, or too much work on hard ground. They are bony enlargements of the splint bone on either side of the cannon bones. Cold water treatment and rest will usually cure any lameness but the splints may need to be pin fired or blistered. A curb, which is a swelling seen below the point of the hock when a ligament has become enlarged, can also be treated the same way.

There are many other ailments of the feet and legs including spavins, ringbones, sidebones, sprained fetlock joints and strained tendons which can be treated by rest and in some cases cold water treatment. Most, however, can be prevented with care and understanding.

# CHAPTER THREE

# Clipping and the correct use of rugs

HORSES TURNED OUT all the year round grow thick coats in winter, and they also roll in mud to give themselves added protection against the weather. Heavy winter coats, however, can be a disadvantage for those horses expected to work because they will sweat too much.

A sweating horse must be dried-off after exercise or it may become chilled. Too much sweating can also cause loss of condition. To prevent this happening horses at grass may be trace clipped. Stabled horses are also clipped out when their coats start to get long, but the type of clip will depend upon the work each horse is expected to do.

Keeping a horse well clipped will do much to help maintain its condition and well-being, and the animal will be able to work longer and faster and with more effect. The horse will also dry off more quickly and be easier to groom, at the same time making any cuts or swellings that much easier to detect.

Horses turned out at grass can also be clipped in the winter if they are expected to do any fast work, but for them a trace clip will be sufficient and they should be given the protection of a New Zealand rug.

With a trace clip the hair on the under surfaces of the throat and body is removed, leaving untouched the hair on the top of the body and the legs. Trace clipping used to be particularly popular with the owners of harness horses, but it is now in frequent use with riding horses and with ponies in particular.

Stable-kept horses used mainly for hacking and other relatively light work may be given a blanket clip, when a little more of the hair is removed. This clip is aptly named because the area usually covered by a blanket is left unclipped along with the hair on the legs. The hair on the belly, neck and head, however, is removed.

A stabled hunter should have a hunter clip with all the hair removed except from the legs, where it is left to give protection against thorns and other minor injuries and ailments like cracked heals and mud fever. The hair beneath the saddle is also left to absorb sweat and to prevent chafing.

Some owners, giving their horses a hunter clip at the start of the season, clip them out completely, which has the added advantage of making the legs of a rather common-looking animal look less hairy than would normally be the case. Leaving the hair on the legs and the saddle patch,

however, does provide extra protection when hunting.

The hunter clip is not as easy as it sounds, because making the saddle patch neat and even on both sides requires great care. A useful method of getting the saddle patch even is to use an old saddle or numnah which can be placed in the correct position and clipped round. The correct positioning of the saddle patch is important because if it is too far forward the horse will look short in the shoulder and long in the back. If, however, the hair is cut straight behind the shoulder and left well behind the saddle, the horse's appearance can be greatly enhanced, a point worth remembering when showing or selling a less than perfect animal. Clipping a horse really well without any unevenness or tell-tale clipper marks requires skill and practice and is a real art.

The winter coat is usually given its first clip in early autumn, but, as the hair will probably grow very quickly, it may be necessary to clip again within three months or when the coat is a centimetre or more in length. It is important, however, that the last of the winter clips takes place before the summer coat has started to come through.

The summer coat, being fine and short, should never be clipped, except if a horse has a very thick coarse coat which may then need to be trimmed to prevent it from getting too hot.

The person clipping the horse should wear rubber boots for the sake of safety; long hair should be kept out of harms way with a net or headscarf. The animal's mane should also be tied in bunches so that it can be kept out of the way while the neck is being clipped. Small rubber bands can be used for this purpose. The tail can be tied up in an old stocking secured with a strand of tape.

Various types of clippers are available. The heavy-duty variety are best if there are a number of horses to be clipped regularly, but standard clippers are quite satisfactory, providing that they are not allowed to get too hot and upset the horse. Electric clippers are the most efficient, while small hand clippers are only useful for tidying up a horse. The old-fashioned type of hand-driven clippers needs two people to work them, and are not very satisfactory.

It is important to make sure that the clippers are well oiled and the blades are sharp. Blunt blades pull the hair and cause the clippers to overheat, making a horse unsettled and more difficult to clip. Some horses have a

*(Top, left) The blanket clip. (Top, right) The full clip. (Bottom, left) The trace high clip. (Bottom, right) The hunter clip.*

natural distrust of being clipped, perhaps because at some time they have been clipped badly, causing discomfort and pain. Firm, gentle handling will usually allay their fears, but if an animal refuses to settle, a twitch may have to be used, particularly when clipping the head. It is better to uses a twitch for a short time to enable the job to be done safely and well, than to allow a horse to become disturbed. In bad cases it may be necessary to ask a veterinary surgeon to administer a sedative to quieten the horse until the clipping has been completed.

The coat must be dry before it can be clipped properly; it should also be free from grease and grit which will make clipping more difficult and cause unnecessary wear on the clipper blades and the motor. The clippers should be used in the opposite direction to the way the hair grows, and the pressure on the skin must be kept as level as possible. To get a line of hair straight do a little at a time; then stand back and take a good look so that any mistake can be rectified before the clip line is too high. This is particularly important when a horse is being trace clipped or blanket

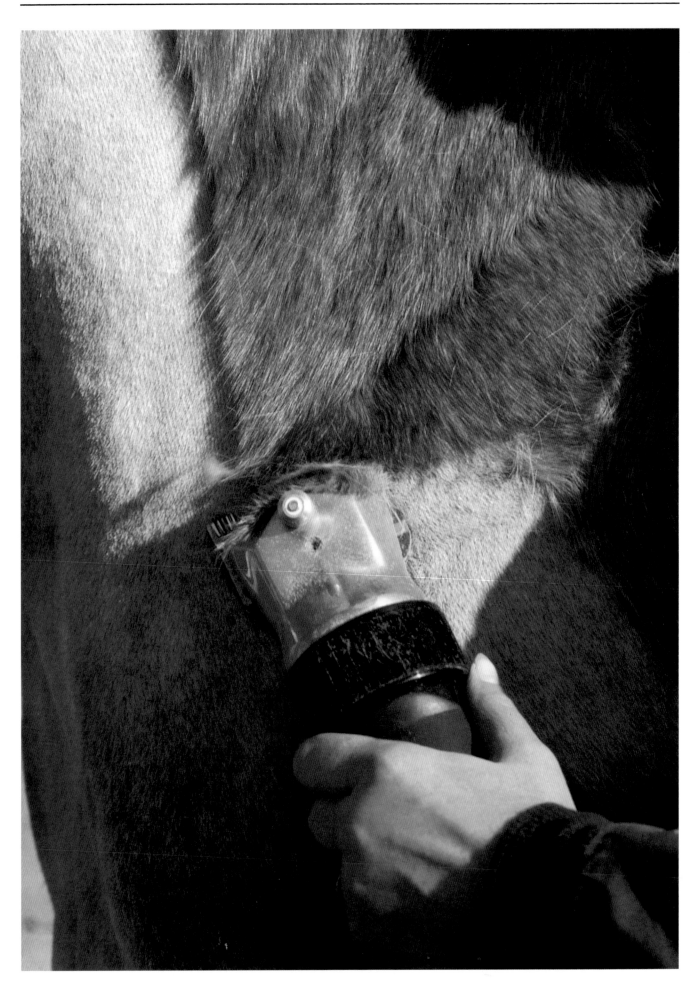

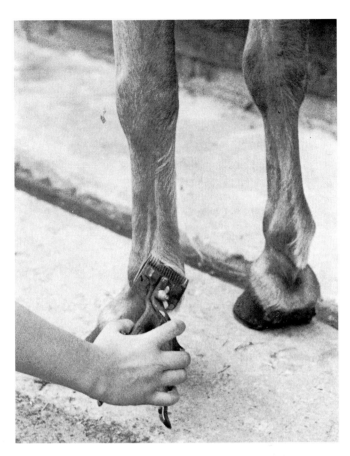

*(Opposite) Patience and experience are essential when clipping. When using electrically operated clippers always wear rubber-soled boots or shoes. Long hair should be kept out of the way with a hairnet or headscarf.*

*(Left) Hand clippers are particularly useful when trimming the heels. The hair growing inside the ears, and the longer hairs in the area of the muzzle, must never be clipped or trimmed.*

*(Below) Pulling the mane correctly will enable it to lie flat. The hairs must be divided and pulled from underneath a few at a time.*

clipped. Always start a little lower than the required height and walk round the horse to see that the lines are the same height on both sides. It is always possible to take a line a little higher if required, but never lower!

Heels can be trimmed barber fashion with the help of a comb and some curved scissors. The hair on the back of the heels, however, should not be clipped too short, or the skin may become chapped and the horse will get cracked heels.

The hair inside a horse's ears must never on any account be clipped. Clipped ears may look smart but the hair is there to keep out flies and insects. If a horse does get a fly

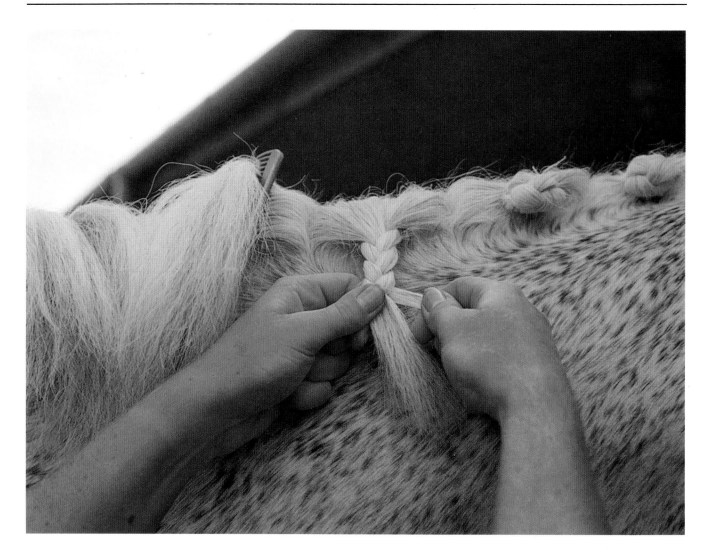

in its ear, it can become very unmanageable and cause a great deal of trouble. The correct method is to trim the hair on the ears flush with a pair of large scissors.

If the weather is cold keep an old rug handy to put over the horse and keep it warm while another area is being clipped. A warm horse will be less fidgety than one that is feeling the cold.

A horse which has just been clipped will also probably feel the cold on leaving its stable for exercise, and be more likely to buck and play the fool. An exercise blanket under the saddle will help, and if an exercise blanket is not available a day rug turned back each side at the front and held in place with the saddle and girth may be used.

In winter a freshly clipped horse will require an extra

*Manes may be plaited or braided for neatness and to show off the neck and crest. Plaiting also helps train the hair to fall into place on the correct side. The number of plaits made along the neck should be of an uneven number, with an additional plait for the forelock.*

blanket under its stable rug or night rug. A heavy type of blanket is preferable because it will go over the back longways under the rug. The blanket can be folded into a point at the front before the rug is put in place, and the point of the blanket turned back over the withers and held in place with the roller. Clipped-out horses must be kept warm and good quality blankets, like really good rugs, are a sound investment in any stable.

# CHAPTER FOUR

# Grooming and skin problems

SKIN DISEASES in horses are far more frequent than many people realise, and in Britain two out of every hundred visits paid to horses by veterinary surgeons are connected with skin complaints of one sort or another. Even that high average doesn't take into consideration the many cases which are dealt with by owners themselves.

The most easily diagnosed group of skin complaints are those caused by parasites, particularly by lice of the sucking and biting varieties. A horse's long winter coat is the perfect place for lice to make their home because the hair provides excellent protection as they burrow down to reach the skin.

Even foals are not immune from attacks by lice, which are attracted by the densely packed hair before the baby coat has been shed. As far as foals are concerned the spring and early summer are the worst times of year, but lice can occur during other seasons, not only in young animals and those kept in fields, but also in stabled horses and ponies.

Lice can be found on many parts of the body, but the mane, neck and sides of the chest are the places to look, and when the hair is carefully parted the lice can sometimes be seen moving over the skin. Even if adult lice cannot be seen the characteristic eggs can be found attached to the hairs.

Because lice irritate, horses can frequently be seen trying to get relief by rubbing their necks, shoulders and tails against posts or other handy objects until the hair is worn away leaving sore patches, which are the tell-tale signs of lice infestation.

In instances of sweet itch, a condition caused by small midges and not by lice, a horse will tend to rub its mane and tail rather than its neck and shoulders. Fortunately sweet itch is not serious and will only occur during the summer months, but, by reason of the intense irritation, it is bad for a horse's well-being and appearance. Apart from baldness where the animal has been rubbing, the skin around the mane and tail becomes thickened. Some animals are more susceptible to sweet itch than others and the disease can be hereditary in ponies which are particularly sensitive to the bites of certain insects such as midges. Whenever possible animals susceptible to the complaint should be kept indoors during daytime when the insects are about, and let out to graze in the evening or at night.

Whereas lice can usually be removed by using one of a wide range of animal insecticides, sweet itch requires a special type of solution, which, although rather greasy, can be quite effective when rubbed into the mane and tail at frequent intervals. Even a greasy mane or tail will look better than bare patches.

Lice, unlike sweet itch, can be readily spread from one horse to another, and if one animal is found to have lice it is important to treat all the horses in close contact, otherwise the condition will never be properly eliminated.

Mange can be caused by four different parasites and may result in slight swellings in the legs as well as causing intense irritation, making a horse stamp and try to bite the affected parts. Fortunately it has now become quite a rare condition.

A very common parasitic disease in horses and ponies turned out to grass in the summer months is warble infection, or bots. Cattle can also be affected. The fly stage is short and the insect does not have a mouth because it does not feed. It simply lays eggs on the coat, usually on the horse's legs, and the horse then licks the coat and transfers the eggs into its stomach. Eventually a grub-type larva works its way to the back of the horse usually in the saddle region during the spring and early summer, causing a swelling. A small hole then appears in the skin allowing the larva to escape and the breeding cycle continues.

Before the larva escapes however the swelling in the skin will be very painful to the touch and the animal will not be able to be ridden unless a ring or pad, with a hole large enough to keep it well away from the infected area, is put under the saddle.

No attempt should be made to squeeze out the grub. Within a few days it will emerge on its own. If it is squashed when it is within the skin a horse which has previously had a warble infection can get a serious allergic reaction, which in extreme cases may prove fatal. There are various methods of dealing with the bot fly eggs on a horse's legs, but probably the most effective is to shave them off carefully with a safety razor.

Fungal infections of the skin are among the commonest complaints encountered by veterinary surgeons. They are generally referred to as ringworm and can be readily passed on to other horses. It is a particularly unpleasant complaint and it can be contagious to humans.

The earliest signs of ringworm can usually be seen around the girth, saddle and bridle areas, because the spores which spread the fungus are easily transmitted from horse

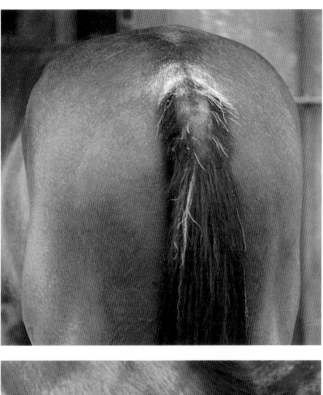

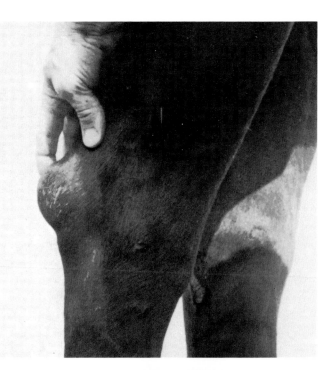

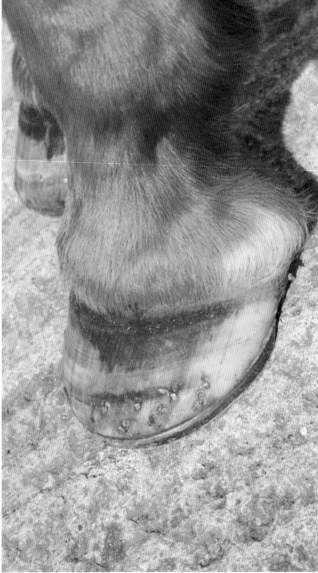

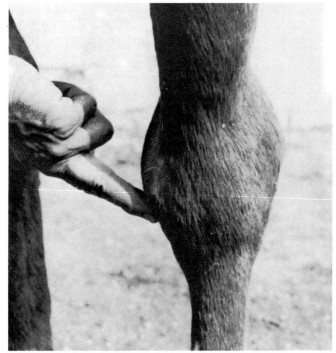

to horse by the saddlery. The lesions start as slightly raised areas which then develop a scaly-crusty appearance and become larger although tending to remain round. Because a number of different species can cause ringworm, a horse may become re-infected quite quickly after being cured, but there are a number of treatments which can be used to kill the fungus and prevent its spread. Antibiotics may be used but it is essential for an infected horse to be kept away from other animals and for saddlery, rugs and grooming equipment to be isolated. People coming into contact with the horse must wash their hands in strong disinfectant to reduce the spread of infection. Ringworm may be encountered at all times of the year. Because it is so

 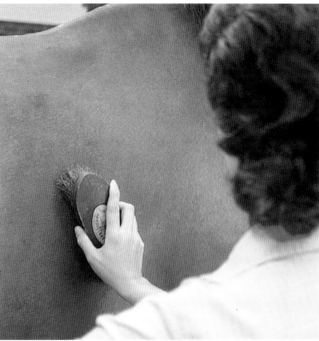

*(Opposite, top left) Sweet itch affects the mane and tail. Horses and ponies susceptible to sweet itch should, if possible, be kept stabled by day during spring and summer months, and allowed out to graze by night when the flies and small midges which aggravate the condition are less likely to be about.*

*(Opposite, top right) Capped hock is a swelling which appears on the point of the hock. It can be caused by a kick when a horse slips when trying to rise. The swelling is unsightly and it is advisable to ask the veterinary surgeon for the best methods of treatment.*

*(Opposite, bottom left) Laminitis (see p. 31) is an inflammation and swelling which is extremely painful. It is brought about by too much heating food and insufficient exercise.*

*(Opposite, bottom right) A bog spavin is a soft non-painful swelling found on the ligament on the inside and to the front of the hock. It is usually caused by strain, the best treatment being rest and cold-water applications. While there is inflammation in the area, it is best to call on expert veterinary advice.*

*(Above, left) Grooming (see p. 42) should follow a planned routine. Begin by picking out the feet with a hoof pick which should be worked downwards from the heel towards the toe. At the same time check that the shoe is secure and that there are no risen clenches.*

*(Above, right) A dandy brush is used with a to-and-fro movement to break up the caked mud, dirt and sweat marks, especially those found in the region of the saddle, points of the hocks, fetlocks and pasterns. Great care must be exercised when using a dandy brush on the more tender parts of the body.*

contagious, in some countries racehorse trainers can be fined if they are seen to run a horse which has evidence of ringworm.

Other skin complaints which may be mistaken for ringworm are those caused by bacteria. A common problem is known as *Staphylococcus* which can cause round raised areas in the skin. There is a scaling scab which does not, however, grow to be as thick as in a case of ringworm, and the trouble can usually be cleared up quite easily by applying the correct type of antibiotic ointment.

Rain scald is an unusual name given to a complaint caused by an organism with the rather impressive sounding name of *Dermatophilus Congolensis*. This organism is frequently present on horses, but will usually only gain entrance to the upper layers of the skin when the coat has been soaked in water for long periods. Because of this it is most often a winter complaint found in horses which have been turned out to grass in very wet weather. Crusty areas appear down the back and quarters with the crusts sometimes becoming up to a centimetre or more in depth. They usually have tufts of hair showing through which in the course of time will separate leaving a bare area of skin. In treating rain scald it is important to water-proof the skin with liquid paraffin which sometimes has sulphanilamide powder added to prevent other bacterial complications.

Girth galls are quite a common problem particularly with rather fat ponies who have very soft skin because they are unfit. Areas of skin, usually around the girth, become thickened and sore, and the animal should not be ridden until the sore patch has healed. If for some reason the pony has to be ridden, a clean piece of motorcycle inner tube placed over the girth in the area of the girth gall will help to relieve the soreness and prevent any friction.

Like their owners some young horses suffer from warts, usually to be found in the area of the muzzle. The cause is a virus which rarely affects a horse after the age of six years, and the warts can disappear as quickly as they arrive. They seem to cause little inconvenience unless they interfere with the bit or part of the bridle which might cause them to become damaged and bleed. When an animal has built

39

Once mud and sweat marks have been removed, the dandy brush should be changed for a body brush (above), with its shorter, closer-set hairs, which can be used in a steady sweeping movement to get the dust out of the coat. (Opposite, top) Most people groom the nearside before moving round the horse to the offside. (Opposite, bottom) The body brush should be kept clean by drawing it sharply across the teeth of a curry comb. When the body and legs have been groomed, attention should be given to the head. Remove the head collar and re-buckle it round the horse's neck. There is now no need for the curry comb, and the spare hand should hold the head still so that the brush can be used gently and with care.

up sufficient antibodies to the virus, the warts will become smaller and eventually drop off. Some horses have warts on other parts of their bodies including the head, neck and legs.

Mud fever is a complaint frequently found in the heels of a horse in wet weather. Horses with white hair on their legs tend to be more liable to this annoying inflammation, although any type and colour of horse may become affected. There is usually puffiness and heat in the legs, and the skin will get sore, rough and scabby. In severe cases of mud fever the animal may even become lame. The legs must be kept dry and free from mud, which usually means keeping the horse in a stable during very wet and muddy weather. If the legs need to be washed they should be dried with a chamois leather or a warm cloth, and the veterinary surgeon will probably prescribe a soothing lotation or cream, such as zinc ointment or lanolin.

Cracked heels can be treated in much the same way. Cracks appear in the hollow at the back of the pastern and the skin becomes red, sore and scabby. If an animal is very susceptible to cracked heels, white petroleum jelly or lanolin should be applied to the heels before the horse leaves the stable.

There are many other skin complaints which can affect horses. Whatever the problem, however, early treatment is to be recommended and the advice of a veterinary surgeon should be sought if the condition persists. Skin care for a horse is important, and stabled horses must have regular grooming with clean brushes to keep their coats in good condition. Horses at grass also need to be checked frequently to make sure that no problem is starting which may cause the animal considerable discomfort and take some time to cure.

# GROOMING – AN ESSENTIAL AID TO FITNESS

Regular grooming (see pp. 39–41) is essential to the welfare of any stabled horse, since the skin is as vital to an animal's health as its lungs or heart. Grooming not only maintains condition, it also ensures cleanliness and prevents disease.

A horse turned out during the winter months grows a long coat which is difficult to keep clean, particularly due to grease and dandruff and the mud which sticks to the coat when the animal rolls.

If a horse which has been turned out is being ridden during the winter months, particularly when the weather is cold and wet, daily grooming should be restricted to a good going over with the dandy brush to remove the worst of the mud. The complete removal of body grease and dandruff with the body brush should be avoided, since both help maintain body warmth and will act as a form of waterproofing of the hair. Its feet should of course be picked out regularly with a hoof pick, and its eyes, muzzle and dock will need sponging with clean water, but that should be the extent of the grooming routine until the weather improves.

Stabled horses however need a regular grooming routine, and people who keep to a system will be less likely to forget any important detail.

The grooming kit should be kept in a box or large canvas bag so that brushes remain clean and can be put away after use in readiness for the next grooming session. Brushes should never be left lying on the ground or they will get damaged and dirty.

During the summer there is no reason why a horse at grass should not be groomed like a stabled animal. A horse moults twice a year, in the spring when a large quantity of hair is shed and the short sleek summer coat is grown, and in the autumn when the short hairs are replaced by the longer and more greasy winter coat.

When a horse is turned out and the weather is really cold its hair will stand on end, increasing the layer of warm air trapped inside, and improving the insulation against the cold. That is why once the coat is dry after a ride it is important to brush out any sweat marks where the hairs have become stuck together, before the animal is turned loose, or the hairs will not be able to stand up properly.

The usual items of grooming equipment are a hoof pick; the dandy brush, which is a wooden-backed brush with strong bristles used to remove the caked dirt and sweat marks; the body brush, which has softer shorter hairs designed to reach through the coat to the skin; the curry comb, used to clean the body brush; a water brush, which also has longer firmer bristles; a mane comb; sponges; two buckets; and a stable rubber.

A wisp, which is a pad made of woven hay or straw, is also very helpful for massaging a horse and developing and hardening the muscles; it will also give a shine to the coat by squeezing oil from the glands in the skin. Wisps do take time to make, and some owners prefer to use a round leather pad which has a strap across the back to enable it to be held more easily. A good saddler will make this type of pad which is a useful addition to any grooming kit.

Grooming should follow a routine which ensures that every part of the horse is dealt with in turn. Begin by taking the hoof pick, that specially shaped piece of metal with a hook at one end designed to remove any stones or dirt that may have become lodged between a horse's frog and the shoe. Picking up each foot in turn, work downwards with the hoof pick from the heel towards the toe. Make sure that the frog, that 'V'-shaped piece in the centre of the foot, is clean, and look for any signs of thrush, an inflammatory

*(Opposite) Sponges are used to clean the eyes, nostrils, muzzle and dock. It is preferable to have two sponges, keeping them continually rinsed in fresh water. One of the sponges should be kept for use on the head, the other for the dock area.*

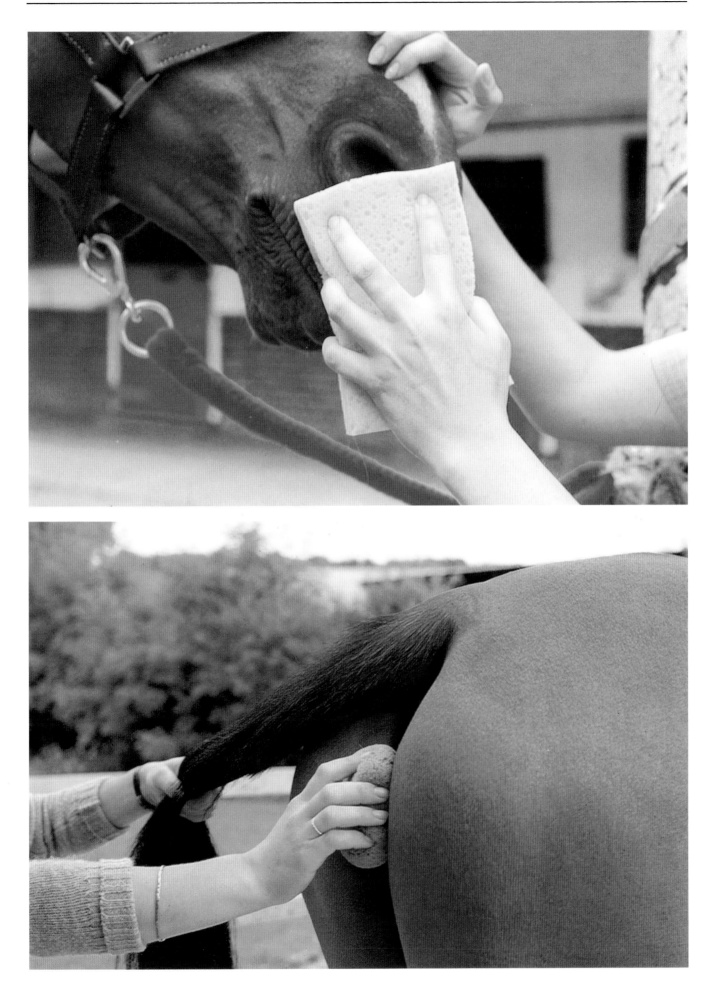

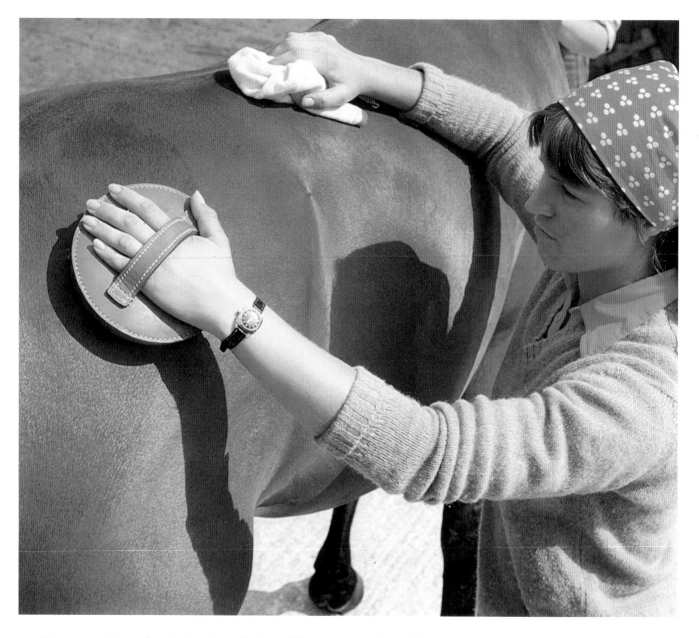

condition sometimes found in a horse's foot. This unpleasant condition is noticeable mainly by a discharge and a rather foul smell.

Next, check that the shoe is secure by tapping it firmly with the handle of the hoof pick. Run your fingers around the side of the hoof to see that all the nails are smooth and none are sticking out to form what are known as 'risen clenches'.

Beginning on the near side at the horse's head, take the dandy brush in the left hand and starting at the top use the brush in a to-and-fro movement to remove all the caked dirt and sweat marks from the coat. Pay particular attention to the parts of the body, like the saddle region, the belly and the points of the hocks and the fetlocks, where the hairs may have become clogged or matted. Changing the brush over from one hand to the other, move round to the other side of the horse. If there is a lot of mud, and the hair is long, a rubber curry comb may be used in a circular motion.

When all the mud has been removed, exchange the dandy brush for the body brush, the main purpose of which is to remove dust and sweat and to reach through the coat to the skin. The body brush is made with short, close-set hairs and is used on the body, neck, quarters and legs. It is also used when brushing the mane and tail.

Grooming should start with the mane. Push the hair of the mane over to the 'wrong' side of the neck, the side opposite to its normal fall, and thoroughly brush the crest. Once this has been completed allow the mane to fall back into its correct position and brush through. Then starting at the head, take a few locks of the mane and carefully brush out any tangles, working slowly down the neck towards the withers.

With the body brush in one hand and the curry comb in the other, the grooming of the body must begin at the neck. The person grooming should stand by the horse's neck on the nearside and work over the entire coat with short, circular strokes, allowing the brush to move in the

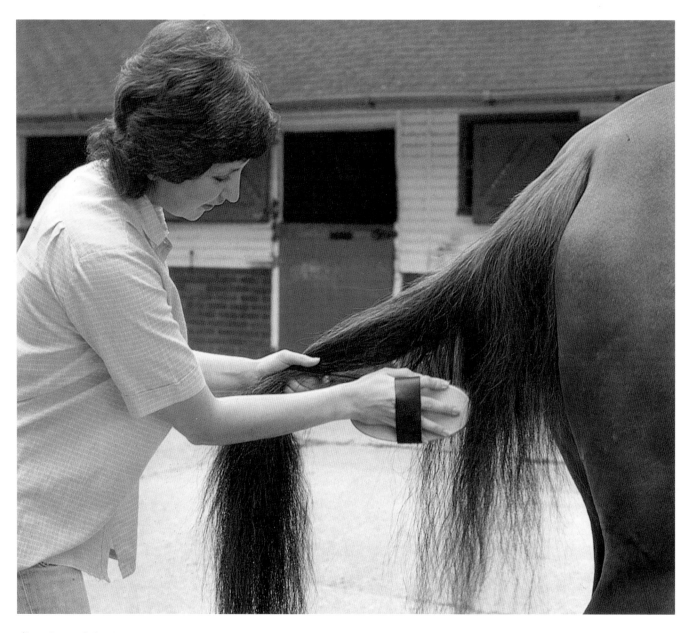

direction of the hair. To do this properly requires a fair degree of pressure, and the weight should be behind the brush. After every three or four strokes draw the brush sharply across the teeth of the curry comb to remove any dirt or scurf which has been collected. This is essential if the brush is to be kept clean and the bristles kept free from clogging. The dust can be removed from the curry comb by tapping it gently on the floor.

When the nearside of the horse has been completed, change over and repeat the grooming of the offside, frequently changing hands between brush and comb as the work progresses.

Once the horse's mane, body and legs have been groomed it is time to move to the head. First remove the head collar, keeping the rope by which it is attached to the ring firmly in position. The head collar, once undone around the horse's head should be re-buckled around the neck to avoid any risk of the horse running off. Horses usually are quite happy to have their heads groomed and,

*(Above) Brush the tail free from tangles and knots by taking a few strands of hair at a time and brushing in a rhythmic downward movement. A body brush should be used – never a dandy brush. Some people prefer to use their fingers.*

*(Opposite) A wisp, made from twisted straw or hay, or a specially made leather pad, makes a great contribution to a horse's well-being after the main part of the grooming routine has been completed. Used with a banging motion as a form of massage, the wisp or pad will help harden up the muscles and improve blood supply.*

provided this is done gently and with care, they will not put up too much resistance.

During the grooming of the head the curry comb will not be in use and this will leave one hand free to hold the horse's head. Immediately the head has been groomed replace the head collar.

To assist in the hardening up of muscles, and to improve blood supply, a horse needs some form of massage. This is

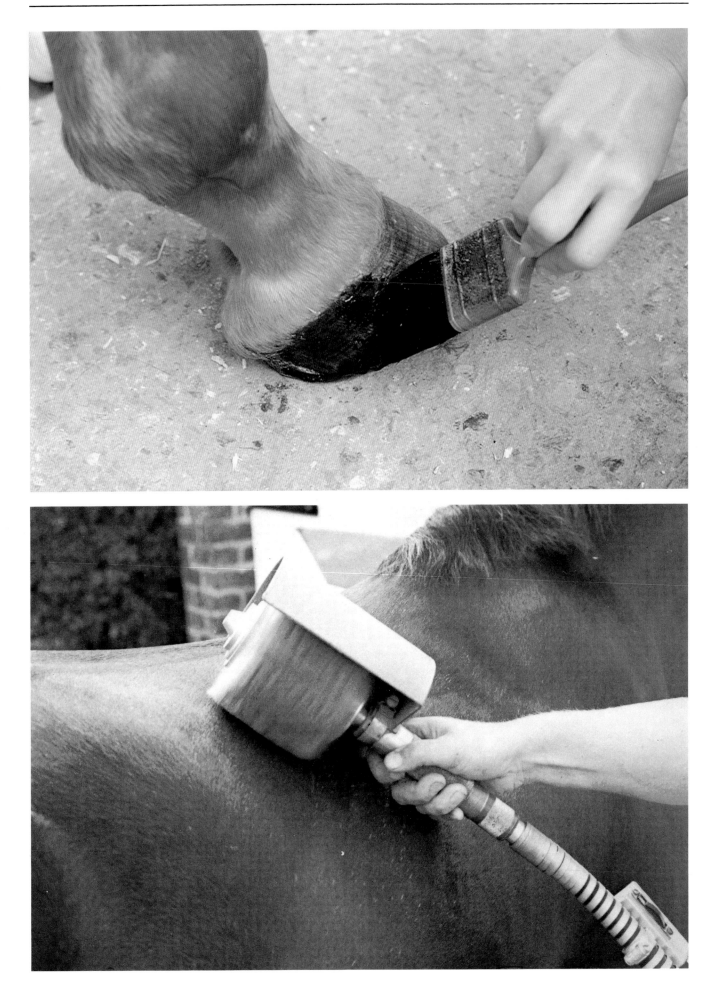

given by the use of a wisp made from neatly woven strands twisted hay or straw. Wisping also produces a shine on the coat, and is a part of the grooming procedure thoroughly enjoyed by a horse or pony.

Before using a wisp, it is preferable to slightly dampen it. To use a wisp, or a leather pad, bring it down vigorously with a 'bang' in the direction of the lay of the coat. Pay special attention and consideration to those parts of the horse's body where the muscles are hard and flat, such as the sides of the neck, the quarters and the thighs, and care must be exercised to avoid the tender regions of the loins. As the wisp is brought down on the coat in a steady rhythmic movement the muscles should be seen to twitch.

At this point it may seem the hard work of grooming is now over – but there are still some finishing touches to be made.

One essential part of the daily grooming procedure is the use of sponges to clean the eyes, nostrils, muzzle and dock area. It is best to have at hand two sponges and two buckets of clean water. Wring out one of the sponges and, holding the horse's head with one hand, gently sponge the eyes working away from the corners. When the eyes and eyelids are clean, and once the sponge has been rinsed through,

*(Opposite, top) Oiling the hooves improves appearance and can help to prevent brittle or broken feet.*

*(Opposite, bottom) Grooming machines are used in some large stable yards to remove mud, sweat and dust. They can be used to speed up the grooming process, but for many owners/grooms a machine can never be as satisfactory as the traditional method of grooming.*

deal with the area around the muzzle, including the lips, and the inside and outside of the nostrils.

Take a second sponge and, lifting the horse's tail as high as possible, clean the whole of the dock area including the skin underneath its tail. This is most important because sponging helps to refresh the horse and it will probably appreciate the sponging more than any other part of the grooming routine.

While a water bucket is handy, dip the end hairs of the water brush in the water and after shaking away any excess lay the hair of the mane flat by brushing it from the roots downwards.

Unless the weather is extremely cold and frosty, the water brush can also be used to wash a horse's feet. When doing so however it is important to keep the thumb of the hand you are using to hold the horse's foot pressed well down into the hollow of the heel to prevent any water becoming lodged there.

When the hooves are dry they will be ready to be oiled. The best way is to use a small clean paint brush which can be dipped in the jar or can of hoof oil. The oil will not only improve the appearance, but will also help to prevent brittle or broken feet.

The grooming sequence has not yet finished, for it is necessary to go over the horse with a stable rubber to remove the last traces of dust from the coat. The stable rubber should be slightly dampened and used in the direction of the lay of the hair.

Finally, the tail must be brushed free from tangles and knots, although some people may prefer to use their fingers to remove the tangles.

Always allow plenty of time. A *complete* grooming will usually take about forty minutes, and if it is to be effective, it must be done thoroughly each day.

# CHAPTER FIVE

# The importance of correct feeding

HORSES and ponies require food to maintain their correct body temperature at 100.5 degrees Fahrenheit; to manufacture tissue; to retain weight and condition; and to provide energy. Too much food for the amount of work to be undertaken will mean excess being stored as fat. This is the major reason why diet is important if a horse is to remain fit and well.

A horse will use its sharp front teeth, or incisors, for cropping when grazing, and its back teeth, or molars, for grinding the food up. Once food passes down the gullet into the stomach, which is comparatively small, the majority of the digestive processes begin to take place, though most occur further down in the digestive tract.

While in the stomach the food becomes mixed with digestive juices before being passed into the small intestine. Here the next digestive process takes place. The small intestine is divided into three parts: the duodenum, the jejunum, and the ileum; it is about twenty metres in length. After leaving the small intestine the food travels to the caecum, and nutrients are absorbed into the system as it moves along.

The caecum is about three times the size of the stomach and this will retain food for some thirty-six hours before being passed further down, into the colon. While in the caecum the fibrous parts of the food are broken down, moving through the system by the contraction and expansion of circular or longitudinal rings of muscle. Bacterial fermentation continues in the large colon until all the fibre is broken down and any which cannot properly be absorbed is passed out in the form of droppings. A healthy horse passes droppings ten or twelve times each day.

Grass is the natural food for a horse, and during the summer months an animal who is turned out will be able to obtain all the necessary nourishment, although during winter months, when the grass has stopped growing and has little or no nutritious value, it will need extra roughage in the form of hay. It will also need additional protein.

Stabled horses require at least three meals each day and their diet should contain the correct balance of water, roughage and energy-giving foods, including protein, starch, sugar, fat, vitamins, minerals and salt.

If a horse has a sufficient supply of water in its stable it is less likely to drink too much after meals. A fully grown horse will drink between ten and twelve gallons of water each day, and buckets are preferable to the automatic stable watering equipment. Using buckets of water, and watching how much is being taken, is the only way a check can be made on the amount of water being taken.

Plastic dustbins, when full of water, can be kept in a corner of the stable and refilled as required. These are less likely to be knocked over, and a lid can be put on a dustbin when it becomes necessary to prevent a horse from drinking for an hour or so before taking strenuous exercise.

Where water is not freely available horses should be watered before meals and never afterwards. A hot, tired horse should be given small amounts of water until it has had an opportunity to cool down.

The most common form of roughage is hay which can contain up to fifteen per cent protein. There are four main types of hay: timothy, clover, mixed, and meadow. Timothy hay is very nutritious, but if cut late, the stalks can be tough and hard to digest. Clover hay is somewhat rich, whereas mixed hay is taken from specially seeded pastures so that it consists of a variety of mixed grasses and clovers. Meadow hay is taken from permanent pastureland and can contain herbs and flowers and other plants which are not always found in new lays.

It is not always easy to tell how good a sample of hay is by taking a handful. A bale, however, should be seen to fall open when the strings are cut, it should smell sweet and fresh, and should not have any signs of mould, dust or damp patches.

Bad hay must never be fed. It is far better to give horses oat straw if good hay is not available. This will contain protein, but barley straw is not recommended since it has spiky 'awns', and traditional wheat straw has little food value.

Sugar beet pulp is also sometimes fed as roughage. Although this has nearly as much protein as oats it has a large percentage of indigestible fibre, and must always be soaked in water before being used.

Oats, which contain all the necessary dietary elements, is the best feed for giving energy. It will also help in building-up muscle. Horses and ponies can eat quite large quantities of oats without their digestion becoming upset, although an excess of oats will make an animal very fresh and full of itself – as pony owners will know!

The colour of oats does not matter providing the grains are short and plump and there are not too many husks. The grains should be heavy to handle and make a rustling noise as they are allowed to filter through the fingers. Oats, whether crushed or bruised, must always be dry and free from odour, and should not be fed to horses until the grain is at least a year old.

Barley is a good food for young horses and those that need to put on weight. It contains slightly more fats and starches than oats but has fewer salts and fibre. Although horses are not as likely to get as excited when fed barley as they can become on oats, barley can be high in nitrogenous elements and for that reason it should be fed with care. It should always be bruised because it is indigestible if the husks have not been cracked, and barley should also be

*Good quality hay is essential for a stable-kept horse or pony and for all animals kept out at grass during the winter. Horses allergic to hay may be fed special nuts.*

boiled and allowed to soak before being put into a feed. During the boiling process the grains will swell to about twice their normal size and become more easy to digest. Boiled barley is usually mixed with bran and other concentrates, and can help improve the condition of horses that have been off colour.

Flaked maize makes a very good heating food in the winter. Because it is very palatable, it is useful for tempting a shy feeder, and it is also useful for putting weight on a horse. Less fibrous than oats or barley, it does contain a high proportion of starches, sugars and fats.

49

To make a bran mash: (Opposite, top left) take sufficient bran to half fill a clean bucket. (Opposite, top right) Add boiling water and mix to give a paste-like consistency. (Opposite, bottom) Sprinkle between 30–115 g (1–4 ozs) salt into the mixture. (Left) Stir well, adding further boiling water if necessary. (Below) Place a sack or piece of towelling over the bucket and leave the mash to cool before feeding.

Peas and field beans are nutritious, but they are also very heating which accounts for the expression that a horse is 'full of beans' when it gets a bit above itself. They should only be fed to horses in really hard work, or to those which have to be turned out in hard, wintery conditions.

Some owners like feeding soya bean meal which is a high source of protein. Similar to peas and field beans, this should only be fed when horses are being worked hard. Even then, a horse should not be given more than .45 kg (one pound) a day.

Milk pellets are a convenient and controlled way of providing protein to horses which are in hard work, but who for one reason or another are not able to be fed much grain.

Pellets are based on skim milk powder and contain protein, vitamins and minerals. They are frequently fed to young stock whose mothers cannot or will not feed them. They are also good for ponies, and will not excite them in the way some other sources of concentrated protein may. At the other end of the scale they are given to horses who have reached an old age and whose teeth may be no longer capable of grinding.

Linseed is another most useful form of food for putting on condition, and for giving a sheen to a coat. It is high in protein and contains oil in a form which is acceptable to a horse or pony. In its natural state linseed contains poison; it must always be boiled before being fed either in the form of a mash, jelly or gruel.

Linseed jelly is an excellent tonic which can be added to normal feeds. The linseed should be cooked for several hours and stirred regularly until it becomes a jelly. Any water which is left can be drained off and used for what is known as linseed tea.

Gruel, excellent for a tired horse, is cooked in the same manner as for linseed mash, and is strained through a piece of muslin to remove all the grain. This should be fed as soon as it becomes cool and before it turns into a jelly.

Root crops, such as carrots, mangolds, swedes and turnips have little real food value, and should be sliced lengthways before being fed.

The concentrates provided in horse and pony cubes or nuts give a ready mixed diet. These consist of various foodstuffs being ground into a fine meal and then compressed into shape. There is a wide range of nuts available, some of which are designed to form a complete diet. Others can be used to supplement short feeds. Complete nuts, and there are several varieties from which to choose, are useful for horses and ponies who are allergic to hay.

Bran, one of the best foods to have in a stable, is a by-product of wheat, containing vitamins B and E. A feed containing bran helps a horse to eat more slowly and to chew more thoroughly. Apart from increasing bulk in a normal feed, bran helps to regulate a horse's droppings. When fed damp it acts as a mild laxative. Fed dry it brings loose droppings back to normal. In the traditional mash form it is easy to digest and will provide an excellent meal for horses who are tired or who have been required to remain in their stable longer than normal.

Salt is an essential additive for horses when the weather is hot or when they are being given extra work. A horse can lose between fifty and sixty grams of salt each day by sweating, and a further thirty-five grams in its urine. If salt is not replaced daily it can lead to fatigue and overheating. A salt lick is perhaps the best method of providing salt, and some licks contain, in addition to the basic element, iron, manganese, cobalt, zinc and iodine.

Every horse will need two and a half per cent of its body weight in food each day in order to maintain condition. This means 1.12 kg (two and a half pounds) of food for each 45 kg (one hundred pounds) of bodyweight. Once the bodyweight has been established it is not difficult to calculate the amount of food required, although horses, like humans, can vary their food requirements and still remain fit.

The weight of a horse can be estimated by measuring its girth and its length from the point of the shoulder to its buttocks at the furthest point. By doubling the measurement of the girth, and multiplying by the length, a figure will be arrived at which should be divided by 300, giving the weight to establish the amount of food required daily.

# CHAPTER SIX

# Saddlery and protective equipment

A WELL fitting saddle and bridle is essential, for unless a horse feels comfortable it cannot be expected to carry out its rider's wishes properly. A badly fitting saddle will not only cause discomfort, it will also hamper the movement of the horse's shoulders, and bring unnecessary pressure to bear on its back.

Horses may look similar in build, but they are never identical in shape. For this reason, after the type of saddle has been selected, it should be fitted by a saddler. It is always best, except in the case of Western saddles, for each horse or pony to have its own. This is the only way a saddle can truly fit, since with use it becomes moulded to the shape of the animal's back.

Western saddles are designed and made in such a way that one saddle will frequently fit a number of different horses, but in the case of European saddles the terms 'general purpose' or 'all purpose' refers only to a type of saddle which may be suitable for a variety of uses. They will not necessarily fit a number of different shapes and sizes of horse.

There is no point in spending time, money and effort on schooling a horse properly, and making sure that it is fit and well, if its performance is going to be spoilt by a saddle which is not comfortable. Pressure and friction are the two most frequent causes of soreness; it is essential to make sure that the framework on which the saddle is constructed fits correctly. The correct name for the framework is the saddle tree which is usually made in three sizes, narrow, medium and broad.

Saddlers can sometimes make a narrow tree a little broader, but they cannot make a broad tree narrower.

Modern trees allow a reasonable amount of flexibility in fitting, particularly with a saddle which has a sloped-back head to keep it off the withers, and small adjustments can be made to enable the saddle to fit perfectly. Apart from freedom of movement for the withers, the saddle must be kept clear of the backbone when the rider is sitting well into the seat. Numnahs and wither pads which fit under the saddle should never be looked upon as a longterm solution for one which does not fit correctly.

Numnahs, which are really pads cut in the shape of a saddle, can become saturated with a horse's sweat, causing overheating and soreness, but if it is decided to use a numnah the types made of plastic foam are best because they are easier to wash and keep clean. Wither pads are more usual in racing stables, although they can be used as a temporary measure if the padding at the front of a saddle has begun to sink, and until the saddle can be restuffed.

There is a wide choice of saddles, from the general and all-purpose types, to show saddles, hunting saddles, military and police saddles, dressage saddles and jumping saddles, all of which are shaped differently, either to show the horse off to better advantage, or to give more comfort to the rider. Racing saddles may weigh only a few ounces, but military saddles and the type used by mounted police are very much heavier.

Whatever the size or shape of the saddle it will require a good strong girth to hold it in place. These can be made of leather, webbing, lampwick or nylon cord, and vary in length from 92 cm (3 ft) for a small pony to 1.35 m (4 ft) for a large horse. A leather girth is best, providing it is kept clean and supple, but stretchable webbing girths are extremely good, particularly for riding across country.

Modern stirrup leathers are made of cowhide, rawhide or buffalo hide. All leathers will stretch, but cowhide leathers are best, having less elasticity. New stirrup leathers should be allowed to settle before being used for competition work, and the near and offside leathers will benefit from being changed over fairly frequently, otherwise the nearside leather will become longer due to the rider's weight when mounting.

Stirrup irons made from pure nickel are unreliable since they may bend, but those made of nickel mixtures or preferably stainless steel are smarter, and more dependable.

There are five main types of bridle. The most common is the snaffle, but the Pelham, the Weymouth or double bridle, the gag and the bitless bridle are all in common use. Inexperienced riders having difficulty in controlling a horse may feel that a more severe bit would solve their problem, but often the reverse is the case. A more severe bit in inexperienced hands can cause pain, and a horse's usual reaction to pain is to pull harder. In an effort to ease the pain and evade the action of the bit the horse may also try to cross its jaw, throw up its head, lean on the bit, or put its tongue over it, making the animal much more difficult to control.

Horses who tend to take a rather strong hold frequently go more kindly in a plain snaffle because it will probably

cause less discomfort in the hands of an inexperienced rider. There are, however, some horses which are not really novice rides and will need a stronger bit. It is seldom easy to find the best bit for a horse without some experimenting.

Having found the right type of bit, care must be taken to ensure that it fits correctly and is the correct width for the horse's mouth, otherwise its proper action may be impaired.

Although European bridles may be used with different types of bit, they all have a headpiece which includes the throatlash to prevent the bridle from slipping over the horse's head; cheek pieces which buckle onto either side of the headpiece and hold the bit in place; a browband which prevents the headpiece from slipping; the cavesson, or noseband; and the reins.

The exception is the single rein bitless bridle, of which the Hackamore is probably the best known. This has two

long metal cheeks, curved to embrace the nose by means of leather attachments which act on the chin and the cartilage of the nose. This type of bridle is of Mexican origin, and is sometimes useful when a horse has a mouth injury which does not allow a normal bit to be used. However, in the hands of a bad rider a bitless bridle can cause great pain.

There are various types of Pelham bit which can be used in conjunction with a curb chain, and to which the majority of horses will react very kindly. The most popular are the vulcanite or rubber mouth Pelham, the Scamperdale, and the Kimblewick which has become a favourite for children. The Kimblewick has a short leather strap buckled on each side to join the upper and lower loops which allows a single rein to be used instead of the usual double reins.

The best type of double bridle for the less experienced rider consists of a Weymouth bit with a sliding mouthpiece and a short cheek, used in conjunction with a plain snaffle.

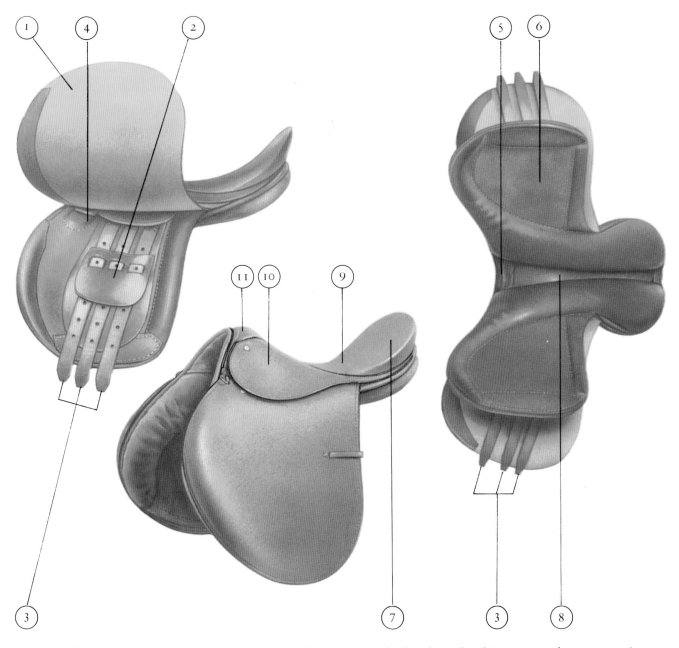

*(Above) The names given to various parts of the saddle are: 1 Saddle flap; 2 Buckle guard; 3 Girth straps; 4 Point pocket (part of the saddle tree); 5 Gullet; 6 Sweat flap; 7 Cantle; 8 Panel; 9 Seat; 10 Waist; 11 Pommel.*

*Two saddles: (Opposite, left) a general or all-purpose saddle; (Opposite, right) a dressage saddle showing the straighter flap.*

This combination of bit will encourage a horse to relax his bottom jaw in response to the rein.

Fitting the bridle is important. With a snaffle bit on its own, the cheek pieces should be adjusted until the bit touches the corners of the horse's mouth without wrinkling them. In the case of the double bridle the snaffle should also touch the corners with the other bit lying just below. The curb chain can be fixed to the offside hook and turned in a clockwise direction until all the links lie smooth. The chain can then be given another half turn to the right and placed on the nearside hook at the length required. The chain must lie flat along the chin groove when pressure is put on the curb rein. If the links are not flat they will chafe the jawbone and cause considerable pain. A chin strap should be placed through the centre loop of the curb chain and fixed to either side of the Weymouth bit to prevent the chain from riding up. When the reins are slack there should be adequate room for three fingers to pass between the curb chain and the jawbone, and the curb should only be brought into action when the cheeks of the bit are drawn back to an angle of 45 degrees.

There are various nosebands which can be used with the different types of bit. The most common of these is the cavesson which is buckled above the bit and under the cheekpieces of the bridle. The cavesson should be adjusted until it is buckled to about two fingers' width below the cheekbone, yet remains loose enough to allow two fingers to be placed between the noseband itself and the jaw of the horse.

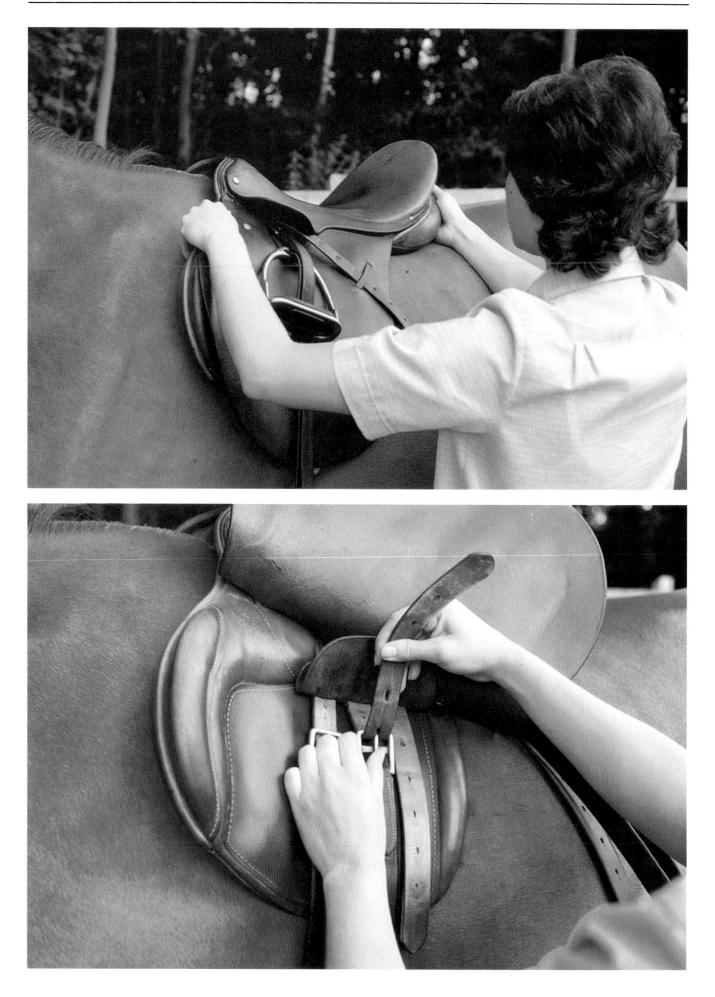

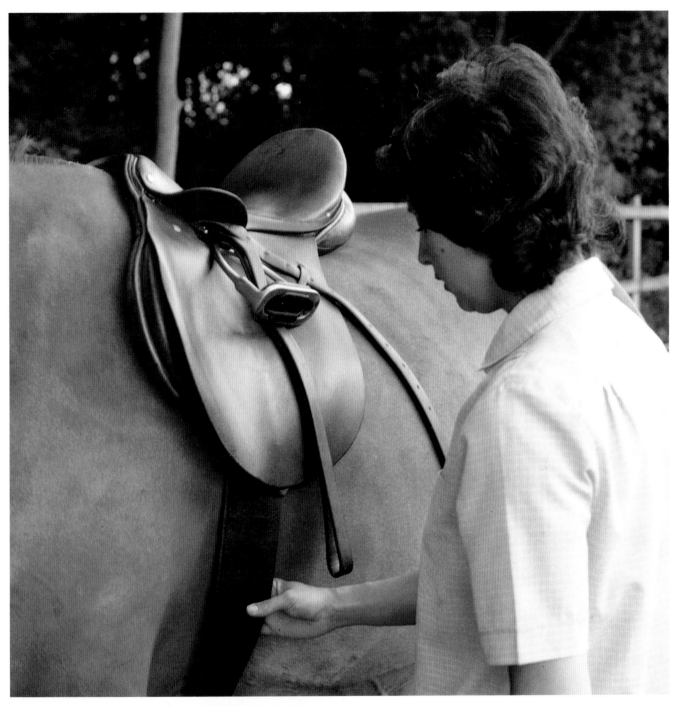

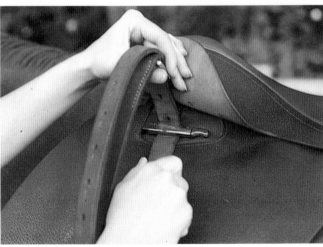

(*Opposite, top*) *A saddle being put on from the nearside at the highest point of the withers, then carefully brought back to its correct position.*

(*Opposite, bottom*) *The girth is buckled sufficiently to ensure the saddle is secure.*

(*Above*) *Check the tension of the girth before mounting because the horse may have 'blown himself out' when the saddle was first put on. If the girth is too loose, the buckles should be tightened evenly and the buckle guard pulled down over the buckles to prevent wear.*

(*Left*) *Stirrup leathers are held in place on the saddle by the metal stirrup bars.*

57

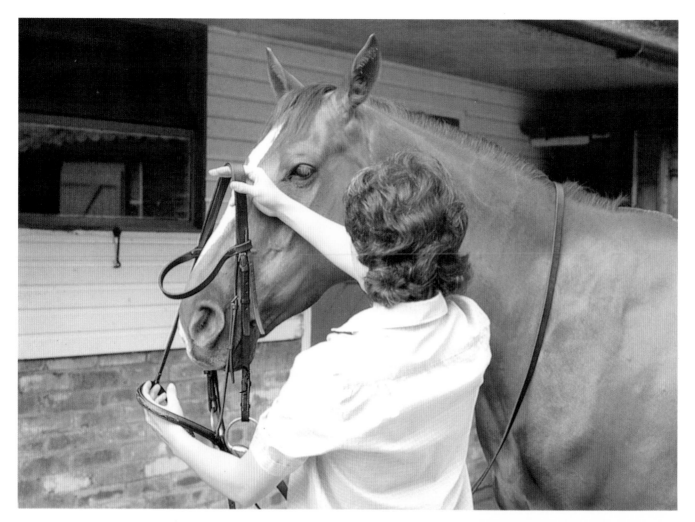

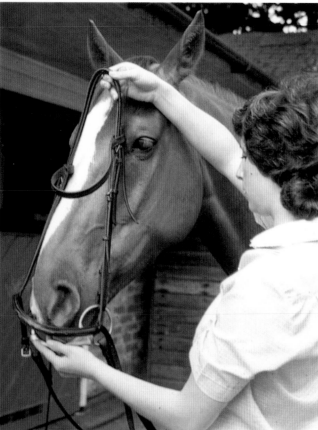

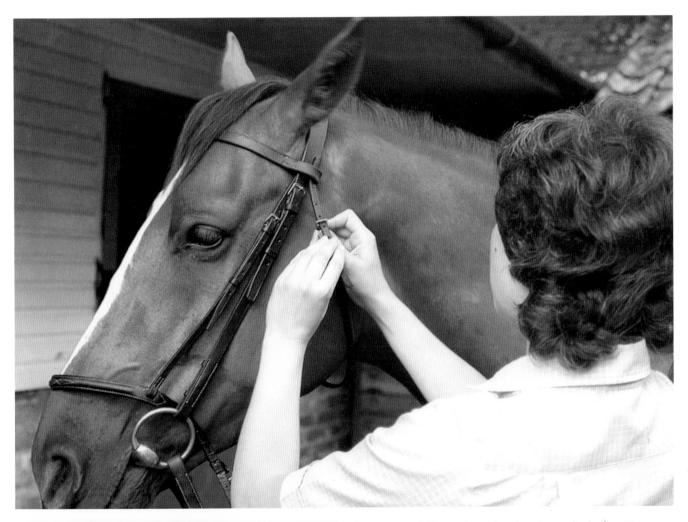

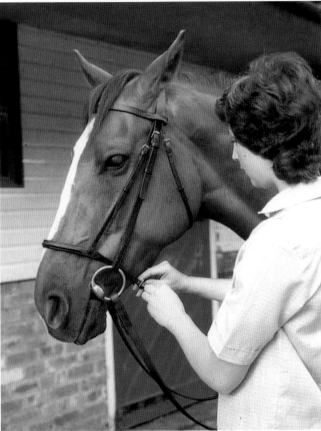

A sequence of illustrations showing the method of putting on a snaffle bridle. (Opposite, top) Hold the mouthpiece in the left hand and the top of the bridle in the right hand. (Opposite, bottom left) Ease the bit into the horse's mouth. (Opposite, bottom right) Place the headpiece over the ears. (Above) Buckle up the throat lash before attending to the noseband. (Left) See that the bit and noseband are correctly positioned.

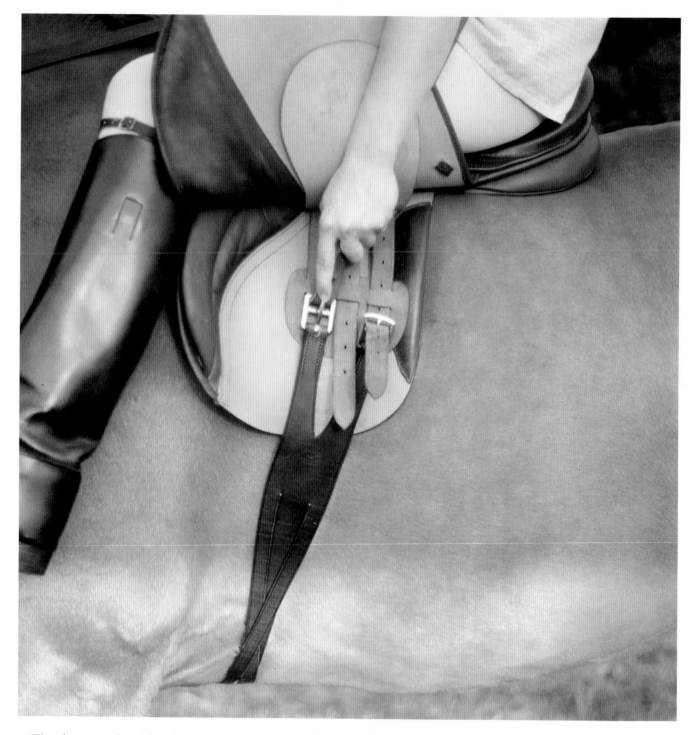

The drop noseband has become popular, particularly among show jumpers, and is used to stop a horse from opening its mouth or crossing its jaws. The bottom strap of the drop noseband buckles below the bit, but the front of the noseband must be high enough to prevent any interference with the soft part of the horse's nose which is extremely sensitive. A Grakle noseband, which has also been made popular by show-jumping riders, is another type of double noseband designed for a horse that reaches for the bit with its mouth wide open, or one who swings its head.

A crupper is rarely used with riding horses, but is useful for rather fat small ponies which are narrow at the front,

*(Above) Having mounted, check the girth again. Some further adjustment usually has to be made before moving off.*

*(Opposite) The rider's seat, showing the position of hands, legs and stick.*

making their saddles inclined to slip forward. It is a leather strap which is attached at one end to a 'D' at the rear of the saddle, and has a loop at the other end which goes under the tail.

Martingales are popular with many riders, although good hands will go a long way towards eliminating the need for them. A standing martingale, which is fixed by a loop at the girth and strapped at the noseband, will help to

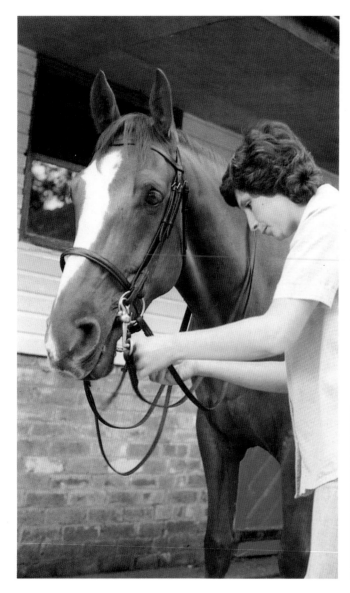

control a confirmed 'stargazer'. It should be adjusted until the horse can raise its muzzle to the level of its withers, but no higher, so that the martingale will not impede normal movement of the horse's head and neck, or prevent it from extending itself properly when jumping.

A running martingale is usually considered more suitable for jumping, because it is firmly fixed only at the girth and allows more freedom of movement. The two straps at the other end of the martingale have rings attached for the reins to pass through. Another is known as the Irish martingale, or the Irish rings. It is a short leather strap with rings at each end through which the reins are passed to prevent them from going over a horse's head.

# PROTECTIVE EQUIPMENT

Horses need some form of protective clothing, particularly when they are competing, in the same way that sportsmen and women often take precautions to save themselves from knocks and strains.

Protective equipment for horses falls into three different categories: clothing to keep a horse warm or to protect it from the flies; bandages and boots to protect it when travelling; and different types of bandages and boots to help protect it from knocks, cuts and strains during competitions.

In cold weather horses will need rugs and blankets to keep them warm. If clipped, or thin-coated, when turned out during the winter they will need a New Zealand rug which is waterproof, and usually made from stout canvas and lined with blanketing. It is not intended for use in a stable, but will enable a stabled horse to be turned out into a field for an hour or so when the weather is not too cold.

The New Zealand rug is the same shape as a normal stable rug, and usually has one or more straps at the front which are secured by buckles. There are additional straps at the back which cross over each other and pass round the horse's hind-legs to hold the rug in position when the horse gets down to roll. These straps round the hind-legs must always be undone first when the rug is being removed or they can become tangled round the horse's legs once the

*(Opposite, left) Fixing the curb chain of a double bridle.*

*(Opposite, right) A Grakle noseband, named after the horse that won the Grand National steeplechase in 1931. Today, the Grakle is in wide use.*

*(Above) A flash noseband which, like the Grakle, (see page 60), is a variation of the standard noseband. The bottom straps are fastened under the bit as the illustration shows.*

*(Right) Over-reach boots to protect the heels of the forelegs from the over-reaching of the hindfeet. The illustration also shows the position of brushing boots.*

other buckles have been undone. Some New Zealand rugs also have a surcingle to help hold them in place.

Because these rugs get hard wear, not only from the weather but also from the horses brushing them against branches and hedgerows, they need regular attention. Tears must be stitched to prevent rain getting through to the warm layer of blanketing; leather straps will need greasing to prevent them from getting too hard, thereby causing chafing, and buckles and fastenings need to be oiled. Some New Zealand rugs are also equipped with hoods which can be fitted in particularly bad weather.

Stabled horses cannot exercise themselves in their boxes to keep warm in winter months and will need a night rug or a stable rug made of jute and lined with blanketing.

When the weather is cold a blanket should be put under the stable rug. A heavy type of blanket is best because it will be less likely to work loose.

Most stable rugs need to be held in place with a roller. These should be well-padded, so that they will fit snugly over the back and not press on the spine, and they should have buckles which do up at the nearside. The cheaper rollers are made from hemp, wool or jute web, but the more expensive are made of leather. Rollers should always be fitted very carefully to ensure that they do not press down too heavily on the horse's spine in the vulnerable area behind the withers. A roller which doesn't have sufficient padding will need a piece of foam rubber underneath until it can be re-stuffed.

Rugs can be purchased in various sizes depending on the size of horse. They all need periodic washing or dry cleaning and the better quality rugs last longer and will look better. When not in use rugs should be stored in a suitable cupboard or large box along with some moth balls or similar protection.

Day rugs are not essential, but they do look smart, particularly when a horse is being taken to a competition. They are made from thick, coloured woollen fabric bound with a contrasting coloured braid, and usually have the owners initials sewn in one corner. Like the stable rug they are kept in place with a matching surcingle or roller, but the day rug also has eyelets at the rear so that a braided tail string can be used to help keep the rug in place and prevent it from sliding forward.

A more important rug is the anti-sweat sheet which is used not only in the stable when a horse has been brought in sweating, but also at a competition, when it can be put over a horse which is hot so that it can be walked round to cool down. These rugs are made from large cotton mesh and work on the same principle as a string vest. By creating air pockets next to the horse's body, they create a form of insulation which prevents it from getting chilled. They can be used with a top sheet or summer sheet and are held in place with a roller to prevent them from becoming dislodged. Summer sheets are made from cotton or linen and are useful for keeping dust or flies away from a horse either in the stable or when travelling.

Horses do not really need any other form of protective clothing when in the stable except for bandages which can be put on the legs of a cold horse to help get it warm, or used to keep a poultice or other form of leg dressing in place.

When horses are travelling, however, there are many items of equipment which can be used. Apart from travelling bandages on the legs, a horse will need a tail bandage to prevent the top part of its tail from becoming rubbed when it is in the horse box or trailer. This is a thin, flexible bandage which must not however be put on too tightly particularly if the tail is damp. A tail guard made from thick woollen cloth or soft leather, can be put on over the tail bandage. It is secured in place with tapes and an adjustable leather strap running from the top of the tail guard to the roller.

A head guard may be needed to protect a horse's poll in case it bangs its head against the roof of the horse box or trailer. This is usually made from padded leather or foam rubber with ear holes and is sometimes known as a poll pad. If a proper poll pad is not available, and there is a possibility of a horse striking his head, either cotton wool or a piece of foam rubber wrapped round the headpiece of the headcollar and held in place by a stable bandage will give some protection.

Knee caps and hock boots are other valuable items of clothing for protecting vulnerable areas. The knee cap, which can also be used when a horse is being ridden on the road, consists of a strong, stiff, leather pad, set in fabric. At the top there is a leather strap which buckles fairly tightly above the knee and prevents the knee cap from slipping down over the knee. It is well-padded at the front to enable the strap to be tightened safely. The lower strap, however, should be buckled loosely below the knee so that it will not prevent the joint from bending normally, but will stop the knee cap from turning upwards.

Hock boots are rather similar to knee caps in that they are fixed and below the joint, and buckled above the hock. They are used to prevent injury when a horse backs up hard or suddenly against the back of the box.

Although stable and travelling bandages are made from woollen fabric or flannel, the exercise and working bandages have a degree of stretch so that they must always be put on over cotton wool or gamgee tissue.

On the front legs the exercise or working bandages should be positioned between the knee and the fetlock joint. They need to be sewn in place for cross-country riding, or have strips of sticky tape placed over the bows to prevent them from coming undone. Bandages can become loose when a horse is galloping and jumping across country, sometimes with unfortunate consequences.

There are various types of boots to help prevent damage to a horse from knocks, strains and cuts. Brushing boots,

*(Opposite) Leather items of saddlery should be cleaned by first using a dampened sponge to remove any dirt or grease. Saddle soap, which helps preserve leather, is then applied. At no time must leather be 'cleaned' with hot water or any form of detergent. Never place leather saddlery too near heat which would cause the leather to dry out too quickly and would remove natural and applied oils. In nice weather saddlery may be cleaned outside.*

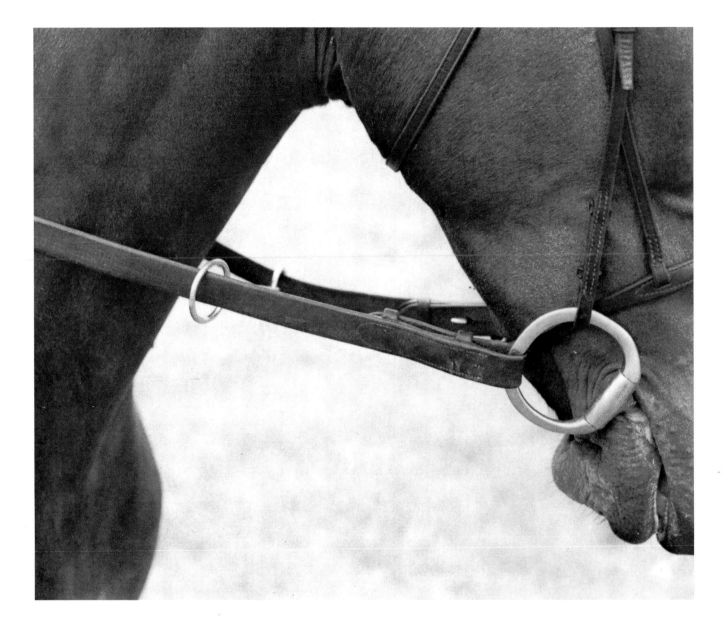

which are made from felt or leather and usually have five straps to hold them in place on the leg, give protection against a horse hitting a foreleg or hind-leg with its opposite leg as it moves. This is known as brushing.

When a horse is jumping or galloping over heavy going its fetlocks may come into contact with the ground. A boot covering the heel can save damage when this happens, particularly when the ground has flints and stones either on top of the ground or just below the surface.

Another problem can be on over-reach, when a horse touches its front leg with its hing-leg, and often when jumping the cut will occur low down on the heel; the best form of protection is the over-reach boot. Made from fairly thin rubber so that it is elastic enough to be easily pulled over the hoof, the over-reach boot must be small enough to fit quite tightly round the foot without moving the leg.

A more serious type of injury can be caused when a horse strikes into itself and hits the joint at the back of the tendon.

Tendon boots have been designed to help reduce this risk, because they are shaped to the leg, and have a strong leather pad at the rear. Show jumpers also sometimes put shin boots on their horses to protect the front of their legs should they hit a fence.

# THE CARE OF SADDLERY

Saddlery must always be cared for properly, not only because it is expensive, but also because every rider has to depend on the bridle, and to a lesser extent the saddle, for stopping, steering and controlling a horse.

Broken stitching or brittle and worn leather can cause problems, and too much water, heat or neglect can quickly ruin even good quality saddlery. Leather loses a percentage of its fat content every day, and the heat and sweat from a horse's body will make leather dry and ready to crack, unless it is cleaned regularly.

Leather has two sides, a grain and a flesh side. When the leather is cured, care is taken to ensure that the natural oil and fat is retained. The grain side of the leather is water-proofed and the pores closed. On the flesh side, however, they are left open to allow the leather to absorb nourishment, so it is the flesh side which needs the most attention when cleaning. The heat and sweat from a horse is not the only cause of leather deteriorating. Moisture and dirt will make it dry and stiff so that it becomes uncomfortable for both horse and rider.

Saddlery should be taken apart before being cleaned, otherwise the dirt and grease which collects in the buckles and keepers cannot be removed properly. A bucket of tepid water and a clean sponge is the most efficient way of doing this, and the leather can then be dried and treated with saddle soap or some other good leather dressing. The saddle soap should be used with a damp cloth and rubbed well into the leather on the flesh side. If the cloth is too wet the soap will bubble and become sticky, but treatment

*(Above) Metal items like bits and stirrup irons should be washed clean and dried before being polished with a duster.*

*(Opposite) Irish rings, one of the types of martingales now in use. The purpose of Irish rings, which are usually used in racing, is to prevent the reins from going over a horse's head in the event of a fall.*

with any good leather dressing will help preserve the stitching as well as the leather.

Poor quality saddlery is difficult to maintain, and almost impossible to repair when it becomes worn or broken, whereas good leather can be made to last a very long time.

Cleaning saddlery properly can be most rewarding. A saddle horse, a bridle hook, and plenty of clean warm water will make the task simpler and quicker. A good stiff hand brush, perhaps an old dandy brush, can be used to brush clean the underside of a linen saddle, and it will also be useful for cleaning webbing girths. Nylon cord girths may

*The New Zealand rug is a strong, lined, waterproof rug which provides excellent protection for a horse or pony when out at grass during winter months. The rug in this illustration is a little too large for the horse, but it is better for a New Zealand rug to be too large than too small.*

be washed in warm soapy water and then rinsed in clean water and left to dry.

Felt or sheepskin numnahs can be brushed, but saddle cloths, saddle blankets, wither pads and foam rubber numnahs really need to be washed from time to time.

Metal items like bits, stirrup irons and buckles should be wiped with a damp cloth, or washed in soapy water and rinsed before being polished with a dry rag. The tongues of the buckles need regular oiling to ensure that they are free to move easily.

The care of leather is an art, and a well-kept saddle room, emitting the refreshing smell of freshly cleaned and oiled leather, is usually an indication of an efficiently run stable yard. Properly treated leather should have a deep sheen rather than a high polish, and saddlery which has a nasty, thick, dark coating of soap, scurf and grease obviously has not been cleaned properly.

Saddles, bridles, and other items of leather saddlery need to be kept in a reasonably warm, dry atmosphere because air temperature and humidity are important. Some conditions have a decidedly adverse effect on leather. A cold, damp atmosphere makes leather absorb moisture and feel nasty and sodden. Artificial heat dries out the natural oils, and a warmish damp atmosphere produces mould which will also damage the leather.

Properly looked after good quality leather rarely breaks, and will remain strong and supple for many years. Stitching, however, should be carefully examined at frequent intervals, because it will deteriorate in time however well it is looked after.

Items of saddlery like stirrup leathers, which are under a considerable amount of strain, tend to give first at the holes; to prevent the leathers from becoming uneven due to the weight of a rider when mounting, they should be changed over from time to time. A good saddler can always shorten the leathers at the buckle end if need be.

Girths and their fixings must be watched for wear and tear and it is also important that buckle guards which fit over the girth buckles should be used to prevent the buckles from wearing holes in the saddle flaps.

Other items of saddlery will also require regular cleaning. Some of the modern head collars are now made of webbing which can be washed if they become very dirty, but a good brushing should be enough to keep them reasonably clean, particularly if the horse is turned out. Leather head collars should be cleaned and saddle soaped in the same way as the bridle, remembering to undo all the buckles beforehand. Head collars do become hard and uncomfortable if they are not kept soft and supple. Ropes of the nylon variety can be washed and hung up to dry, but the safety clips will need greasing.

Rugs and blankets also need regular attention. New Zealand rugs are probably the most likely to suffer damage because they give protection to a horse when turned out. The damage is usually caused when a horse gets down to roll, particularly if the surcingle is loose, or when it brushes against branches or thorns.

Cleaning a New Zealand rug can be done by unfastening all the clips and putting the rug over a fence, or a very strong clothesline, and scrubbing it well with a hard bristled scrubbing brush or an old dandy brush. Scrubbing will not damage the canvas which can be left to dry in the sun or in a drying room. The blanket part of the rug can be brushed, but if it is really dirty it may also have to be washed.

When the rug has been dried the stitching will need to be checked and any tears in the canvas or the blanket lining repaired. A saddler will be able to patch a bad tear in the canvas, but if the rug is reaching the end of its useful life and will soon have to be replaced, a tear can sometimes be mended quite effectively with a patch of strong adhesive tape.

It is important to ensure that there are no tears or holes in the rug which will let in the water, because unless the rug is waterproof the blanket underneath will get wet, and the horse will get cold. If the blanketing is too badly torn it will have to be replaced.

The leather straps that hold the rug in place should be treated with a good leather dressing to prevent them from becoming hard. Apart from being likely to crack, hard straps will rub the hair from a horse, and cause chafing.

Night rugs always get dirty and stained, and washing and drying them can present a problem. An industrial washing machine is the easy answer, but few laundries are prepared to deal with horse rugs, although they can sometimes be persuaded to wash blankets providing the majority of the hairs have been removed with a stiff brush.

It is more usual to wait for better weather and to wash the rugs in a water trough or an old bath and let them dry in the sun or boiler room. Some night rugs have their own surcingles in addition to the breast straps, and apart from checking the stitching the buckles will require oiling.

Day rugs made from wool, like the cotton and linen summer sheets, are much easier to deal with and can be dry-cleaned after the hairs have been removed. Anti-sweat rugs, however, are more difficult to clean being made of large cotton mesh which can tear easily.

All bandages get dirty and must be washed regularly whether they are made from woollen fabric or flannel, or are exercise bandages and tail bandages which have a degree of stretch.

Knee caps, hock boots and tendon boots will also need attention. Those made from felt can be brushed clean, and those of leather must be washed and treated with saddle soap or some other leather dressing to keep them supple. The straps will need checking because broken buckles and loose straps can be very annoying when the boots or knee caps are needed in a hurry.

Saddlery cannot be effective unless it is looked after properly, and the same is true of rugs and other equipment. Time spent on cleaning and maintenance is never wasted.

# CHAPTER SEVEN

# The farrier and the foot

HORSES need to have good feet and be properly shod if they are to be able to do their work well. The old cavalry saying 'no foot – no horse' is as true today as it was when soldiers depended on their horses to carry them in battle and to pull their guns.

It is difficult to realise that horses were never intended to carry the weight of a rider, or to perform many of the other tasks they now do so well. Their achievements are all the more remarkable because a horse's foot is only a few centimetres across and yet it often has to support half a ton of horse and rider, and also take the strain and concussions of a horse galloping and jumping.

Even so, a horse is not naturally prone to lameness. Only when it is asked to carry a rider's weight, or pull heavy loads, over a variety of different surfaces for long periods, and at faster speeds than it would normally travel, do problems of lameness arise.

If a horse has mis-shaped feet, or box-like feet, the animal will obviously be more prone to lameness than one with good strong feet more capable of absorbing the stresses and strains caused by hard ground and modern roads.

It is to prevent horses from getting sore feet and to stop their hooves from breaking and splitting that metal shoes are nailed to the walls or outer part of hooves. These shoes have to be replaced regularly, not just because they will wear out through contact with the roads, but also because they can interfere with the natural growth of the hoof.

Metal shoes are bound to have some effect on the natural functioning of a hoof, but how much effect they have will depend on the skill of the blacksmith or farrier.

Because of the serious nature of foot problems it is important to know something of the structure of the hoof and the way in which it works.

Anyone looking into a horse's hoof, if this were possible, would see a number of bones with layers of sensitive flesh around them. Although the walls and the bottom of the hoof, known as the sole, are rigid, the inner part can have limited movement because of the rubber-like quality of a triangular wedge known as the frog.

It is this triangular wedge at the back of the sole which takes much of the weight and absorbs the concussion when the foot hits the ground. As it does so it becomes pressed down, and then expands forcing the ends of the wall out-wards and enabling the inner part of the hoof to move slightly.

Another reason for taking care when dealing with a horse's feet is the fact that when other parts of the body become damaged, or are subjected to severe concussion or strain, they can usually swell and relieve the pressure. A hoof, however, can only swell very slightly and this inability to swell can create serious complications, which may in very bad cases cause the bones of the foot to become deformed or pushed out of place. When this happens the result may be a horse that is permanently unsound and lame.

The wall, or outer part of a healthy hoof is insensitive and similar to human nails. It grows at a rate of about one centimetre a month. That is why the shoes have to be removed at frequent intervals and the wall trimmed to prevent interference with the natural growth of the foot. When he removes the shoe a good blacksmith will examine it carefully to see if it has been worn down evenly, or whether anything needs to be done to correct a possible fault in the horse's action.

He may ask to see the horse trotted so that he can decide whether a shoe needs to be built up more on one side than the other to allow the horse's weight to be distributed more evenly when he moves.

Before replacing the shoe, or putting on a new one, the blacksmith will cut down the wall of the hoof with a drawing knife and make it level using a large file known as a rasp. When doing so he will be particularly careful not to damage the sole of the foot or the frog. Because the frog is the leg's natural shock absorber it must be able to con-tract rather like a sponge, and to do so it needs to be able to come into contact with the ground after the shoe has been nailed in place.

A shoe must always be made to fit the foot, and the foot must never be cut down or rasped to fit the shoe, or the walls of the hoof will not be able to work properly. Some-times the blacksmith uses what is known as the cold-shoeing method when the shoe is made up beforehand, instead of being heated in the forge and then shaped to the horse's foot. If the blacksmith knows the horse well, and can accurately judge the size of shoe needed, the method can work quite well, but it cannot be as efficient or effective as the old method of hot shoeing.

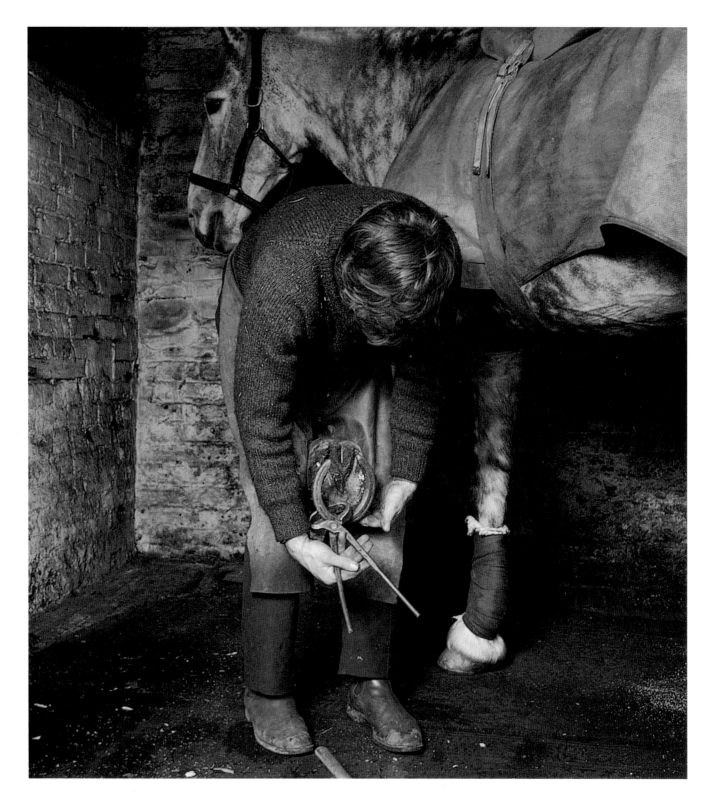

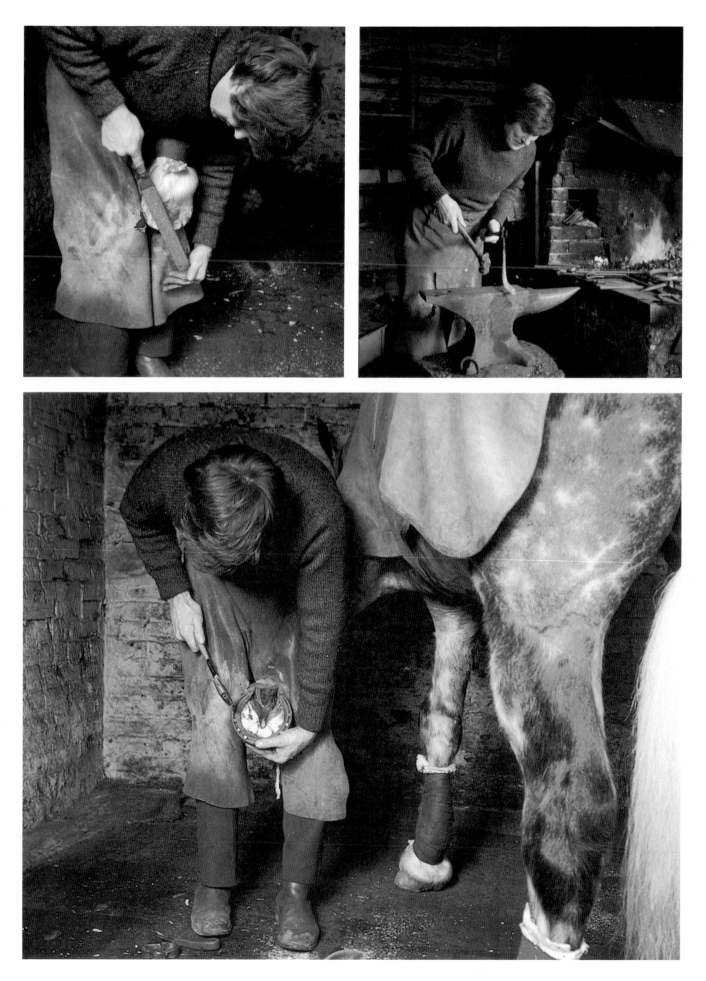

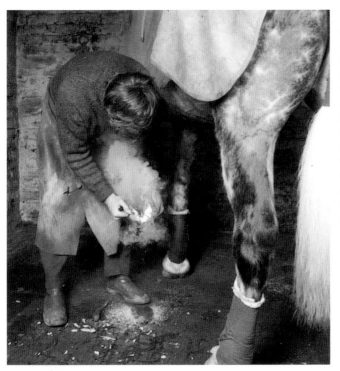

When hot-shoeing a horse the farrier first has to remove the old shoe by cutting off the clenches with a buffer and driving hammer. The shoe is then prised off with the pincers (see p. 71), taking care not to damage the wall of the foot. (Opposite, top left) The foot is cleaned and made level. (Opposite, top right) At this stage a new shoe is being prepared. (Left) The new shoe is taken from the forge and a pointed pritchel is used to hold the hot shoe onto the foot, to enable the farrier to check, by the scorch marks, whether the shoe will fit correctly. (Opposite, bottom) The new shoe is cooled and then nailed onto the wall of the foot, beginning at the toe and working round the shoe. (Below) The nail ends which protrude through the wall need to be twisted off and filed and tapped down onto the hoof to form a 'clench'. The clips will also be hammered into place. Finally the rasp is used to tidy up the hoof.

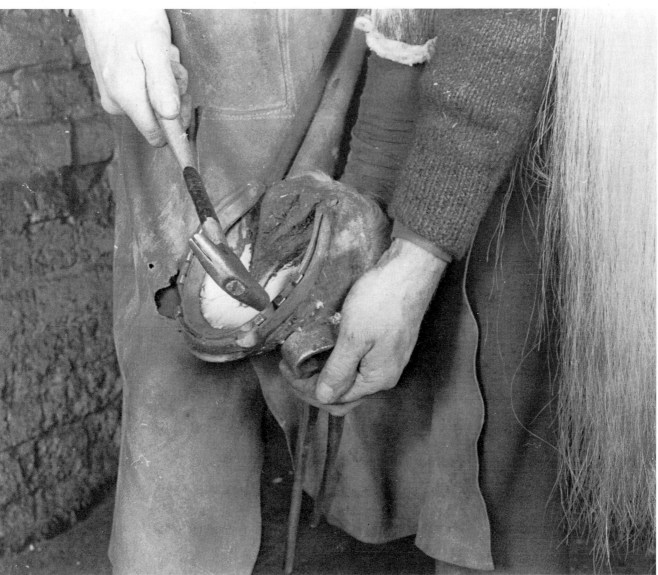

*Horses that compete are usually fitted with shoes which have specially bored screw holes to take studs, which help give a better grip. (See page 81.) The studs are screwed into the shoes with an ordinary spanner. Smaller studs may be used in frosty weather. The holes may be 'plugged' with cotton wool to keep them free of grit and dirt when not in use.*

With hot shoeing each shoe is heated in the forge until it is red hot. Then, by holding it against the hoof the blacksmith can tell whether it fits properly, because if it does the hot shoe will leave brown burn marks all the way round the wall.

After the blacksmith is sure that it is a complete fit, and has made certain that the holes are large enough, he plunges the shoe into a bucket of cold water. Then, starting towards the front of the shoe, he nails it on to the hoof, making sure the nails are evenly spaced.

The clenches, or nail ends, that appear round the side of the wall which he has twisted off evenly, are smoothed off and hammered down before the foot is rasped smooth. It

is very important that the surface of the wall of the hoof should not be damaged in this process, because it is this surface which prevents the horn from absorbing water.

If the nails are not driven into the hoof correctly they will pinch the foot or prick the layers of sensitive flesh round the bones. This can result in blood poisoning or cause an abscess to form. It is of course much more difficult to prevent the nails from damaging the foot if the wall is particularly thin.

Horseshoes are, however, more than just plain semicircles of iron. They usually have clips to help hold them in position. In the case of the front shoes the clip is at the toe but with the hind shoes there is a clip on either side. Each shoe also has a groove running round the part of the shoe which comes into contact with the ground to provide a better grip.

Calkins, which can help a horse to get a better foothold on slippery surfaces, are made by turning over some of the metal at the heel of the shoe to form a sort of small step.

Because shoes can still slide on smooth or icy roads, or slip when a horse is galloping and jumping, studs are sometimes used. Studs are usually four-sided and are screwed into holes which the blacksmith will have made in the shoes. Some of the studs are small and pointed, to be used when the ground is hard; while others are much larger and more rounded, to provide better grip when the ground is muddy and the going is deeper.

When a horse has finished its work the studs can be removed with a spanner, and stored in a box ready for the next occasion. The empty screw holes can be filled with a plug of oiled cotton wool, or some owners use what are known as keeper studs, which fit the holes and prevent dirt from getting into them, as well as protecting the sides where the screw holes have been drilled.

If the threads have become damaged the holes can usually be cleaned out and the threads repaired with a metal 'tap' the size of the stud.

Leather pads, which a blacksmith cuts from a large sheet of leather into the shape of a horse's foot, are sometimes placed underneath a shoe before it is nailed into place. These pads are particularly valuable when a horse has to be exercised in stony country or galloped or jumped across soft flinty ground. The pads not only work as extra shock absorbers on the hard ground, but also stop the sharp flints from cutting up into the sole of the foot causing lameness.

It is easy to appreciate why an experienced blacksmith is such an essential member of the team needed to keep horses fit and well.

# CHAPTER EIGHT

# Exercising and schooling

EXERCISING and schooling a horse is very important to its overall well-being, both mentally and physically. The right amount of exercise will ensure that the horse remains fit and healthy and in a genial frame of mind. In addition, schooling will make it supple and obedient.

It is important to remember when exercising that no two horses are the same, and that there can be no hard and fast rule concerning the duration of exercise periods, or indeed the frequency of schooling sessions.

The biggest factor to be taken into consideration when working out an exercising routine is the psychology of the horse. Horses are like young children in that they become very easily bored which can result in disobedience and loss of temper. For this reason the horse's routine should be varied as much as possible.

A horse who works in a relaxed and happy manner is the sign of a good trainer who has taken great care over understanding the character and temperament of that particular horse. Some horses are very quick to learn while others need a lot of patience and time before they fully understand what is required of them. Very highly strung horses often become excitable and difficult to manage if they are schooled for too long at one stretch. Schooling sessions should never be long drawn out affairs. It is far better to school for five or ten minutes every day, followed by an enjoyable hack, than to school for an hour and make a horse thoroughly bored and bad tempered.

Some horses, however, will need slightly longer schooling sessions because they may take ten minutes or so longer than others to settle or loosen up; half hourly sessions two or three times a week would probably prove more suitable.

With all horses, however, the principles should be the same; never go over the same thing again and again;

*An outdoor schooling area with a specially prepared surface suitable for use in all but the most severe weather conditions.*

always try to vary the sessions as much as possible; and always reward the horse when it has done well. Horses basically like to please and if they are rewarded for something they have done well they will usually be only too happy to do it again.

The amount of exercise will depend not only upon the temperament of the horse, but also upon its state of fitness and the work that it will be expected to do.

The competition horse will obviously need more work than a horse that is used just for general hacking. Unfortunately there can be no short cuts to getting a horse fit. A lot of hard work is involved, sometimes in very cold wet weather, but this is a vital stage in producing a horse which is ready and able to use itself to the best of its ability.

A horse that has been turned out for any length of time, whatever the reason, will need a period of steady walking to begin with, and that usually has to be done on the roads. Six weeks of road work is adequate, although if the horse has had a history of lameness, or has been rested for a year

*(Above) It is essential that an outdoor arena is properly laid down and that the drainage is effective. In this illustration it will be seen that the material which covers the foundation, lying below the actual schooling surface, has been broken and cannot do the job for which it was designed.*

*(Opposite) The surface of an outdoor arena must be raked regularly after use.*

or more, it is advisable to give it up to ten weeks walking to prepare it for the faster work to come.

Once a horse is fit it will obviously have a great deal of energy, and this can become a problem when schooling. The horse may find it very difficult to concentrate and control all its energy, and it is a good idea to lunge the horse completely free. It may take the horse just five or ten minutes on the lunge before it settles, or it may take half an hour, but this is well worth doing as it can avoid an argument in the schooling session.

However, a horse should above all things be obedient, and obedience is something that must be taught from an early age. Even older horses, however, can be 'reformed' with patience and understanding. Horses must be taught to obey the rider's wishes, wherever they may be. Every horse must learn to go where the rider tells it to. It must learn to go away from other horses and to go calmly and sensibly when on its own.

When a horse refuses to go where the rider wishes it is known as 'napping'. This should be dealt with very firmly because it can lead to rearing and other forms of evasion.

If, when the horse first attempts to nap, it is reprimanded immediately, it will be less likely to do it again. However, an older horse who has been allowed to get away with disobedience in the past may prove more obstinate. In such cases great tenacity and endurance will be called for from the rider. Once the horse realises that it cannot get away with being disobedient it will usually think twice before doing so again.

The same principle applies to disobedience when jumping. If the horse refuses at a fence, provided it has not been overfaced, the animal should be hit once smartly behind the saddle and presented at the fence again.

This procedure may have to be repeated before the horse clears the fence, but when the horse does it should be rewarded so that it realises what is expected of it. Horses

*(Above) A horse being lunged at a walk. Note the position of the whip in the right hand with the lunge rein in the left.*

*(Opposite) A cavesson noseband, with rings, for use with a lunge rein.*

must learn to jump from obedience, because in competitions they may be faced with types of fences that they have never seen before, and if they always want to stop and have a look first, they will never be successful in competitions.

Every type of horse, regardless of whether it is to be used in competitions or not, will benefit from schooling. Elementary schooling can improve balance and manageability. The dressage horse can benefit from jumping as it makes the horse use its back, and the jumper will become more balanced in its approach to its fences after training on the flat. The horse that is used only for hacking or hunting is also improved by becoming a more controlled and therefore a more enjoyable ride.

Schooling on the flat makes a horse more supple, athletic and responsive to the rider's wishes, and also serves to strengthen the animal and build up the right muscles.

The horse must first learn to accept the rider's leg aids and to move forward smoothly and freely. The horse must learn to accept the bit; to take hold of it without pulling and to maintain a rounded outline. The rider should, by using his seat and legs, ask the horse to use its hind-legs to create the impulsion or forward-driving force and movement, while at the same time keeping its head in the correct position and maintain a soft, supple, flowing rhythm.

Rhythm is most important and it cannot be achieved without correct balance.

Some horses have natural rhythm and balance, but in most cases the rider must establish them. This can be achieved by keeping the horse calm and relaxed and by encouraging it to keep going forward. Lungeing will help because it will make the horse learn to find its own balance and not rely on the rider to create it.

Some horses increase their speed when they feel unbalanced, intensifying the problem. When this happens, the horse should be restrained and made to realise that balance and rhythm are more easily achieved by a slower pace.

Horses must learn to become balanced at the trot before being asked to canter. Work done on a completely loose rein is very helpful. This encourages the horse to stretch its head and neck and use its back and stops it from leaning on the rider's hands through the bits and reins.

Once the horse has developed calm rhythmic paces, it can be taught suppling exercises like shoulder-in, rein back and the half-pass. These exercises not only increase the

horse's agility, but also enable the rider to introduce more variety into the schooling sessions.

When horses are bored they become sulky and unresponsive, and this can lead to disobedience and evasions. By continually circling, turning and changing pace the rider can keep the horse alert and interested. He must always be sensitive to the horse's condition; if the horse seems to be moving with less spring and impulsion it is likely that it is getting tired, and in that case the rider should stop. If the horse is made to keep working when its muscles are aching this can sour the horse and lead to muscle strain and lameness.

After a schooling session the horse should be taken on an enjoyable hack or turned out in the field for a short time, or if possible both. This will help the horse relax mentally and will keep it in a calm happy frame of mind, especially in the case of a highly strung individual.

The useful place to school a horse is in a specially built manège because this will provide perfect conditions with a

*The illustration opposite shows an experienced horse and rider at a schooling session in an outdoor manège.*

*(Below) Fitting studs to a shoe to give additional grip when jumping or moving over soft or heavy going.*

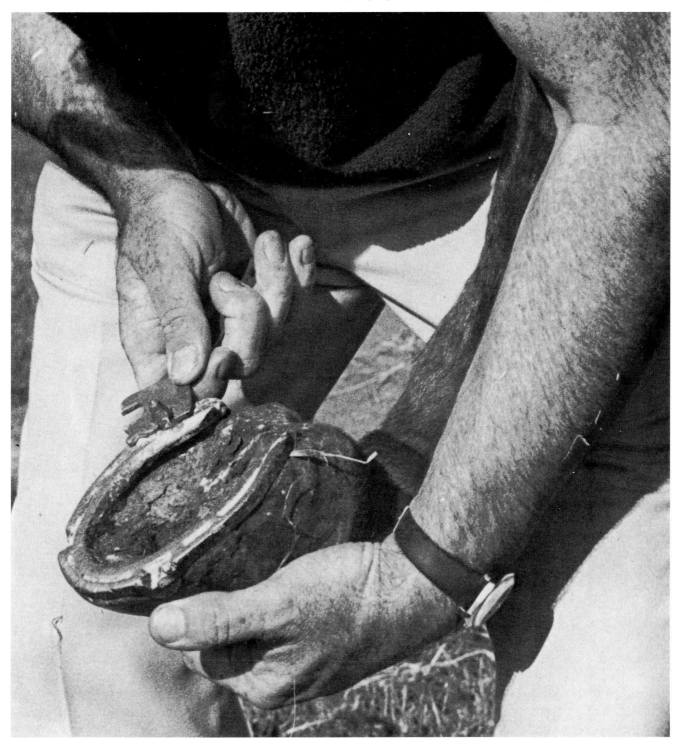

flat surface and smooth even going. It encourages free-moving horses as they do not have to be wary of holes or ruts or false pieces of ground.

A horse that is worked in soft or uneven ground will appear to be unlevel and will be discouraged from moving freely or extravagantly, so that even when it meets good ground it will still 'go short'.

An outdoor school or manège will also mean that the schooling sessions are not totally governed by the weather, because they can be used after very heavy rain or a light frost.

Another advantage of an outdoor manège is that it is easier to make a horse concentrate on its job than if it is being worked in an open space; this makes the task of lungeing both easier and safer as the horse cannot run off.

However, horses must become accustomed, not only to all types of going, but also to concentrating and working in large open spaces where there are other distractions; so even if an outdoor school is available, horses should also be worked in a field to enable them to learn to cope with all types of terrain. Unfortunately, competitions often do take place on unlevel ground and, therefore, a horse must learn to keep itself balanced even when the going is very uneven.

Perhaps the ideal facility for schooling is in an indoor school, with all the advantages of an outdoor school, and the added attraction of not being affected by any weather.

Horses can continue to be worked even in the event of snow and ice, something which is obviously of great importance when keeping a horse fit.

Every horse must learn to be adaptable to conditions and situations, and the same applies to the rider. Variations in exercise and surroundings will keep the horse alert and responsive, but it is up to the rider to keep the interest and to make the horse's work stimulating and enjoyable for it on every possible occasion.

*A plan drawing indicating some of the variety of schooling and exercising movements that are possible in an outdoor school or manège area. The most satisfactory measurements for a manège are 20 m. (22 yds) × 40 m. (44 yds).*

# CHAPTER NINE

# Jumping and cross-country riding

ONE OF Britain's most successful trainers, and a former champion jockey, Fred Winter, summed up the feelings of everyone involved in schooling horses when he said 'All horses can jump – in different ways'.

Whether dealing with steeplechasers, hurdlers, show jumpers or eventers, the principle remains the same: every horse is different – in ability, temperament, action and character.

There are horses that are natural athletic jumpers and always seem to meet every fence perfectly, because they are quick to make adjustments. Others, sometimes because of their conformation, need to be taught how to jump and to make the best of their natural ability.

Some horses love jumping, others lack confidence; some are bold and fearless, others are suspicious and like to know exactly what it is they are being asked to jump.

*(Below) Trotting poles which have been carefully spaced on the ground are a useful schooling aid. Depending on the horse or pony's stride the distance between each pole will require adjustment.*

Horses can best be taught to jump either completely loose, or on the lunge, but they should always be allowed to start to learn to jump naturally without a rider. Even two- or three-year-olds can enjoy trotting over poles on the ground and progressing to small, simple fences. If they start at an early age, they will come to think of jumping as an every-day occurrence and be far less likely to become excitable later.

By learning to jump without a rider the horse learns to think for itself and to sort himself out. The horse can take its time and learn to adjust its stride coming into a fence

*(Below) A young rider makes parallel jumping look easy, but this is perhaps the most difficult obstacle found in a showjumping arena.*

*(Opposite, top) Trotting poles can be usefully positioned in front of a practice fence to encourage a horse to arrive correctly at the point of take off. Note: the cross poles in this illustration do not have a ground line; a ground line should be included when younger or novice riders are schooling.*

*(Opposite, bottom) A young rider taking a low wall during a training session.*

without meeting with any interference from a rider. This is very important because young horses can easily lose confidence and enthusiasm if they are constantly being 'jabbed' in the mouth when going over a jump.

A horse jumping completely loose will very rarely hit a fence, whereas with a rider it can become careless, because a rider, in trying to 'help' may upset balance and distract the horse.

Some horses jump much better if the rider sits still, keeping the horse going on an even balanced stride. Others, however, need to be 'placed' at a fence, and it is the mark of a good rider to know instinctively how much help a horse needs.

After a horse has started to jump confidently over small fences either on the lunge or loose, and has become balanced in its ridden work on the flat, jumping lessons with a rider can be introduced. The ridden lessons should

*(Above) A young competitor taking a fence at a West-Country Hunter Trials.*

*(Opposite) Alison Bradley, a most successful younger rider, here on Monsieur Le Vet, at the Royal Windsor Horse Show in 1989.*

start by just trotting the horse over a pole, so that it can get used to having to rise at a jump with weight on its back. The horse should always be given plenty of rein so that it can stretch its neck and head and not feel restricted in any way. It can then gradually progress to a small fence, jumping it at a trot and canter.

Once the horse is jumping a practice jump with confidence, other small fences can be introduced, so that it learns to tackle a variety of different obstacles. Never make

*Mr Philip Johnson and Puck seen jumping at a recent Burghley Horse Trials in England.*

the mistake of over jumping the horse by continuously jumping the same fences.

Most horses enjoy jumping, but it is better to do a little each day rather than involve them in long drawn out sessions.

The most important rule is never to overface a horse. This applies not just to the size of the jump, but also to how difficult the jump is to negotiate. A small combination fence can prove more difficult to a young horse than a bigger straightforward single fence.

Whenever a horse is introduced to a new problem, such as a combination or a ditch, the jump should always be made quite small so that it can easily 'fiddle' its way over it if necessary. Nothing is more likely to turn a young horse against jumping than making it become frightened. If a horse has learnt to be obedient and to trust its rider it should jump a strange fence at the first time of asking, and must learn to do so early on in its training.

The variety of fences to be found on many cross-country courses today is so great that one is almost sure of coming across at least one type of fence that the horse has never encountered before, and it will not have time to stop and have a look before deciding whether to jump.

Because of this the horse must quickly learn to go when and where the rider tells it. In return, the rider must build up the horse's confidence by never overfacing it and by giving it every encouragement to jump.

If the horse refuses, it should be hit with the stick once behind the saddle as a sharp reminder that it has done wrong, then circled and brought into the fence again.

After a young horse has learnt to jump single fences, it can be introduced to small courses. In the beginning it is a good idea to plan the course so that the horse has to turn after every fence before approaching the next one. This will prevent the horse from increasing its speed too much between the fences. If a horse has learnt to rush its fences, it is a very difficult habit to correct. Small combination fences – two fences with one or two canter strides between them – will make the horse think and increase its agility.

When the horse has reached the stage of jumping calmly and confidently over courses at home, it will be ready to be taken to some small competitions. The first few shows should be used to give the horse experience. Indeed, it is sometimes a good idea to use the first show to let it see the sights and give it a chance to settle down. The horse should be ridden quietly round the showground and allowed to take a good look at everything. Then it can be schooled for ten minutes and perhaps be allowed to jump a practice jump a couple of times before being taken home.

Next time the horse can take part in a small competition, always making sure that the jumps are well within its capabilities. The horse will probably still be so busy looking at everything that it must be able to jump the fences easily for it to gain confidence. Remember that this is the stage when a horse should be learning and getting experience rather than setting out to win.

If the intention is for the horse to become a show jumper there is nothing to be gained by taking it into big competitions before it has had an opportunity to learn its job. Equally, the most important time for an event horse is the novice stage. A season spent going carefully round novice horse trials will stand it in good stead later.

Riding across country successfully is basically learning how to get from the start to the finish safely in the shortest time. It is no good going flat out, hoping that the horse will be clever enough to stay on its feet. Even if this works once, the chances are that the next time the horse will not be so keen and may even refuse to jump at all, and who can blame it? The real art of good cross-country riding is to know exactly when to push on and exactly when to go a little slower.

Good cross-country rounds begin before the competition even starts – when walking the course. That is the time when the rider must decide exactly where to jump each fence and tries to find the shortest route. There are many important aspects to be taken into consideration when walking a course. The rider should start by considering the type of horse being ridden. If the horse is experienced, it might be possible to save time by jumping the most difficult part of a fence instead of taking any easier alternative route. If the horse is very inexperienced then it would be best to make its task as simple as possible, and let it jump the easier, but probably more time-consuming, alternatives.

The state of the ground must also be taken into consideration. Rain can cause deep or slippery going and turn even an easy straightforward fence into a hazard.

Natural hazards on the course must always be looked for; it is important to watch out for drainage ditches, rabbit holes and tree roots, especially in sections of woodland and patches of deep going. Any of these can cause nasty falls, which, although they may go unpenalised if they are outside the penalty zone, can however result in injury to horse or rider.

Consider also where the crowd will be. Many fences look totally different when surrounded by people. Remember that the horse will not have seen the fence beforehand, and quite often spectators can obstruct the view that the horse would normally have of a fence.

If there is a water jump, it is advisable to walk through it on foot before the start to test the depth and to make sure there are not any holes.

The position of the sun can also cause problems. If it is a bright sunny day the rider should try to estimate where the sun will be when they are actually going across country. Bright sunlight or shadows can make a fence difficult to judge.

The position of the next jump should also be carefully noted. Seconds can be gained after every fence if horse and rider set off immediately on the shortest route to the next obstacle.

Once the decision has been made where to jump each fence, it is a good idea to walk the course again, following the exact route it is intended to take.

However, it is not enough to know exactly where a rider wants to jump each fence; things are always likely to go wrong! The horse might not be jumping as well as usual; it might find the ground too heavy or too firm, or it might simply be having an off day. In any of these cases, it often pays to take a few easier alternatives instead of jumping the difficult parts, and so it is advisable to consider both the difficult and the easy alternatives when walking the course.

A good cross-country rider must be flexible, but positive. He must make quick decisions, be in tune with the horse, and able to feel when the horse is tiring or losing confidence.

The type of fence to be jumped must always be considered, because speed should vary according to the type of obstacle. A straightforward single fence can be taken with very little adjustment of pace, whereas combination fences such as coffins, sunken roads, bounces and drop fences need to be tackled at a slower pace and off a shorter, bouncier stride.

The most important thing in any cross-country round is to establish rhythm and keep that rhythm throughout. A rider who can keep up a good steady pace will make much better time than one who attempts to go at a flat out gallop between the fences and then has to check for every jump. Vital seconds can be wasted at each fence in this way.

It is always disturbing to see a tired horse being pushed along by an unfit rider, bouncing up and down on the saddle with flapping reins. A good rider should never try to take a horse faster than it is capable of going. Doing so will lead to jumping mistakes and possibly a fall. He should try to keep his weight off the back of his horse by leaning forwards and taking the weight on his knees, and by keeping the animal balanced and giving it all the encouragement he can.

# CHAPTER TEN

# Preparing for competitive riding

MOST people who ride regularly have at sometime or another had an urge to take part in a competition. It does not matter so much whether they come last, or if they are competing in the handy pony class, or the open jumping – it is the participation and the feeling of achievement that provide the pleasure.

Winning is, of course, a spur to greater achievements, and although it should never become the only reason for competing, it is usually the ultimate objective of any rider.

Competitions, however, are not only won and lost in the few minutes that the horse and rider spend under the scrutiny of the judges. The secret of all success is in the preparation and in the close attention to every detail.

Plans for any competition begin with the publication of the regulations and dates, and careful note should be taken of the close-of-entries date and the rules regarding classes. Horse shows, hunter trials and events not organised or affiliated to the official bodies usually set their own date for the close of entries and these may vary according to the wishes of the organisers.

Entries for horse trials run under the auspices of the country's governing body – the British Horse Society in Britain – are slightly different in that there is both a ballot date and a closing date.

Most events are so oversubscribed that late entries are rarely accepted and many event organisers have to ballot out some unlucky entries in order to leave a manageable number for the officials and judges.

Organisers will usually only accept entries on official entry forms and these are usually attached to the schedules. Entry forms should always be double-checked to make sure that the right horse has been entered for the right competition, and that it has the necessary qualifications.

The day before the competition is just as important as the day of the competition itself. This is the time to collect all the necessary equipment together, for both horse and rider.

At any show or competition, correct riding clothes must be worn, and these vary according to the type of event. The standard riding wear at most European competitions is breeches or jodhpurs worn with long riding boots or jodhpur boots; a collar and tie or a stock; a hacking jacket or a black jacket; and, most important of all – for the safety of the rider, a hard hat.

The most important moments in the life of any competition horse are those vital minutes when the horse is actually competing and putting into practice all it has been taught; it is then that the horse's experience and ability will be judged. It is no good if a horse proves to be brilliant at home, but puts up a poor showing when it really matters.

However, success really lies in the weeks or even months of preparation for a competition; in the hours spent in ensuring that horse and rider are fit and ready to do themselves justice.

The fitness and schooling programme of a competition horse will, of course, depend to some extent on the particular equestrian sport in which it is to participate. Whether showing, dressage, show jumping, horse trials, racing, driving or polo, the horse must arrive on the day in peak condition if it is going to be successful.

The success of the show horse will depend almost entirely upon the way it looks and behaves, and upon the smoothness of its paces. Because of this, great emphasis must be placed on the horse's turnout, grooming, and schooling. Show horses need to be in excellent condition, and compared with racehorses they sometimes look positively fat! Training is geared to building up muscle and in improving overall appearance rather than stamina. A show horse which is 'racehorse' fit will not carry enough condition for the show ring and will be more likely to fidget and misbehave when it should be impressing the judges with good manners.

Dressage horses need to be extremely fit in order to be able to do their job properly. They must be strong and supple in order to perform the often complicated and difficult movements required of them. They also will look better in the eyes of the judges when carrying a lot of condition, and their training is geared to building up their muscles, and making them stronger in their movements. Training a dressage horse is made more difficult because it must be fit enough to perform with zest and enthusiasm while at the same time remaining calm and obedient. It is not easy to get the correct balance between the two.

Show jumpers can be all shapes and sizes providing they have the necessary courage and jumping ability, and they probably work the hardest of all competition horses.

*(Opposite) A horse bandaged ready for the journey.*

tiring cross-country phase, and then retain its suppleness and obedience in order to jump accurately a course of show jumps. In addition, an event horse must be bold, but careful and capable of jumping either at speed or at a more sedate pace according to its rider's wishes. All in all it must have a unique blend of abilities.

The training of the event horse is probably the most varied of all and, as a variety of dressage and show-jumping competitions usually form part of its general preparation before the start of an eventing season, it is also perhaps the most useful.

The highlight of the event season is always Badminton, the famous British three-day horse trials which take place in the middle of April. Every top rider wants to win Badminton and aims to bring his or her horse to its absolute peak of condition at that time.

It takes between three and four months to prepare a horse for a three-day event, and preparation for Badminton will usually begin in December. Most event horses are turned out towards the end of October to have a rest and to relax after their exertions of the previous season. This means that when they go back into work for the following season they are usually fat and rather woolly, and that is when the real work begins.

The first four to six weeks of their preparation are spent just walking on the roads. This is dull work, often in the worst of the winter weather, but it is vital as it hardens up the horse's legs after weeks of inactivity. A horse starts off by doing just thirty minutes' walking and builds up to two hours a day over the six weeks.

After the period of road work has been completed, the horse can start trotting, and the schooling sessions may begin. The amount of work done after road work will depend upon the type of horse. A big animal will need to do plenty of steady trotting before it begins cantering, while a lighter built horse can do more work with less risk of straining tendons.

The path to fitness varies according to each horse. Just as athletes map out personal training programmes to suit their own needs, the same must be done with a horse. Temperament is important. Horses that are by nature excitable tend to get themselves fit because they use up much more energy every day than a calmer, lazier horse who has to be made to work.

Some horses, like people, are naturally lean and, if given too much fast work, will lose too much weight too quickly and will begin to look poor in condition. However, horses that tend to be gross will need plenty of work before reaching peak fitness.

Like their owners, horses have an ideal weight for their

Those taking part in top-class competition can spend weeks on the show-jumping circuit travelling from show to show, and they must consequently be tough and resilient. They have to be galloping fit and strong but at the same time carry enough condition to see them through an often arduous season.

The training of a racehorse, however, is geared far more to speed and stamina. They have to be immensely fit in their heart and lungs as well as in their muscles, and their training will include regular periods of fast work, although the amount done will vary from horse to horse. As with dressage horses, training a racehorse takes a great deal of skill and perseverance in order to bring it to peak condition on the day of a race, and very often to bring it back to that peak for several other races every season.

The event horse has to be a combination of them all. It must be calm and supple enough to perform a good dressage test even when it is one hundred per cent fit; it must be as fit as any racehorse to cope with the long and

size and many racehorse trainers weigh their horses regularly to gauge their progress and make sure they are not losing too much weight. It is important to keep a close eye on the horse's weight.

The training programme of the event horse varies, not only according to the horse, but also according to the temperament of the rider. Some leading riders now use a system which was devised by Jack le Goff, the former trainer of the French, and later the American, three-day event team, which is known as Interval Training. This system of training for horses is adapted from the interval training methods used by some Olympic athletes. It replaces the long gruelling periods of work with several short periods alternating with brief recovery periods. The intervals are timed so that complete recovery is not quite achieved before the commencement of the next period of work. This means that the breathing, heart rate and muscular systems are all gradually improved. Sessions of

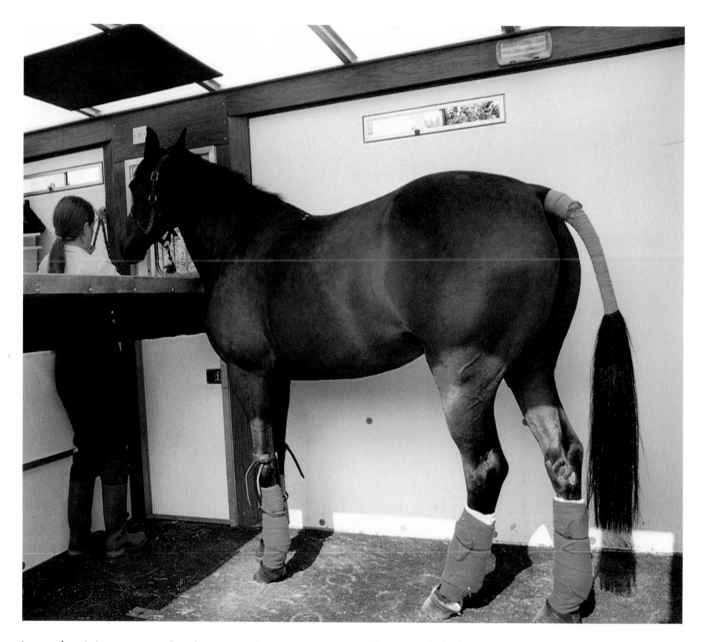

interval training cannot take place more than once every three or four days because that is the time it takes for the metabolism to return to normal.

This method of training can only be used when the horse is sound and completely healthy and has reached a basic level of fitness and condition. It does have three main advantages. It is very flexible and can be varied with each individual horse; it is an efficient way of training, and it conditions the different energy systems of the horse.

Interval Training, however, does not suit the temperament of every horse, or rider. Some horses find the routine too boring and become stale.

Schooling sessions should never be too long and should be supplemented by an enjoyable hack, and where possible, short periods of freedom when they can have a good roll and graze. Horses will enjoy learning if they are treated properly but they need to be given time to digest new information.

In *Equitation*, the British Horse Society's official manual

*(Above) Inside the horsebox there is plenty of headroom and the horse is not cramped. If cramped, the horse may panic during the journey.*

*(Opposite) Jane Holderness-Roddam on Warrior taking the Trakehner when winning the Badminton Horse Trials.*

of training (published by Threshold Books in association with the B.H.S.), there is sensible, sound advice. The book is in two parts: one, dealing with the training of the rider and the second with the training of the horse. The former is so important and so frequently ignored. An outline of the principles and the program of Interval Training is included.

The training programme will also depend on the surrounding countryside. Plenty of hills will make the job of getting a horse fit much easier. The weather and the state of the ground can also affect a training schedule.

Fast work on hard or very heavy ground should always

be avoided as it is one of the quickest ways of laming a horse. Although it is always inconvenient to have to interrupt a horse's training programme because of the weather, it is far better to walk the horse for a week than to continue fast work and probably end up with a lame animal.

Competition horses do not need to be galloped every day, and to do so would be very inadvisable. Some horses do need more fast work than others, but in most cases two days of fast work a week should be enough, and care should always be taken not to overstress the horse. Doing so will only do more harm than good. A good trainer will always try to be flexible and sympathetic to the horse's condition. A horse which seems to be a little jaded should be given a couple of easy days and be allowed to do something different. The animal may have had too much schooling or be feeling the effects of too hard a gallop, and a change of routine would probably do it good.

A competition horse is an athlete and like human athletes its diet is also of great importance. At the start of the horse's programme, when it is just walking, it should be having mainly bulk food, but as the work increases so the bulk food should give way to more energy giving food. As always, feeding should vary according to each individual horse.

A very excitable horse is often made worse by a lot of

*(Above) In an arena set out on level ground in a quiet corner, this dressage test is taking place in almost perfect conditions. The peaceful setting gives every opportunity for horse and rider to concentrate and to enjoy their test.*

oats and is usually better when fed mainly on nuts. The horse may also be liable to lose too much weight and so its diet can be supplemented by flaked maize, flaked barley and boiled barley, which will help to keep plenty of condition on it.

A big horse, that tends to be gross, will need to be fed mainly on oats and chaff with a little bran as roughage. Correct feeding is vitally important and good quality hay is essential. Some owners tend to feed horses as much hay as they will eat, while others feel that a fit horse needs very little. Usually a horse that puts on weight will need very little hay, while a thinner horse can eat more without affecting his fitness.

In the case of event horses, once schooling sessions have been introduced, dressage and show-jumping competitions can be used to supplement the regular training programme. By spring the horse should be ready to take part in some hunter trials to help to sharpen up both horse and rider before the event season begins. Some horses need one or two outings across country before they reach peak fitness and it will be advisable to take them fairly steadily at the beginning of the season.

The days leading up a competition are very important. The last of the fast work should be done at least three days before the event, although most horses benefit from a short 'pipe opener' the day before. Legs should be closely watched because a tough cross-country or show-jumping course could prove disastrous to a horse with legs showing any sign of stress or strain.

The diet needs to be changed, and the amount of hay given the day prior to the competition reduced. Any large amount of bulk foods must be avoided.

On the day of the competition care should be taken over the travelling arrangements, and the way in which a horse is expected to travel. Competitions have been lost before the start by a horse arriving lame after being injured in the horse box through lack of care. Horses must always be bandaged on their front and hind-legs, both for protection and support on long journeys. Knee caps should be worn because horses can slip going up or down the ramp, and a tail bandage or a tail guard is also required. Some horses travel very badly and constantly move around in a horse box; in their case hock boots are also advisable.

Horses can take a lot out of themselves when travelling. When there is a long journey it is often preferable to travel them the day before the competition so they can spend the night recovering from the journey and come out fresh on the day. A horse cannot produce its best if it arrives at the event tired and upset after hours of travel, and months of hard work will be wasted if the horse is rushed into action as soon as it arrives.

Provided everything has been done to ensure that horse and rider are fit and properly prepared for the day all that should be needed is that extra bit of ability and luck.

# CHAPTER ELEVEN

# Show jumping

IN RECENT times, certainly during the years since the end of the Second World War, show jumping has become a highly skilled sport, offering to many, young and old, novice or international, the opportunity to enjoy a variety of jumping competitions. The tens of thousands of horse shows staged each year throughout the world attract an enormous and enthusiastic following.

Some horse shows, to attract a public, intersperse jumping classes with displays, including performances by the military, the police and dogs, as well as quadrilles and exhibitions of riding technique. Most displays have a connection, however tenuous, with the world of horses and riding.

Other shows are staged entirely for the benefit of competitors, and showing and show-jumping classes fill the rings from early morning to dusk.

The rapid development of the sport can best be measured when it is realised that only a few shows were put on between the time of the first recorded competition in the 1860s and 1939. For some ninety years those who competed were faced with somewhat sketchy rules and the sport was barely noticed by anyone. Even the Royal International Horse Show, which opened at Olympia in London in 1907, had an intermittent run until it was revived in 1946.

Even though the Fédération Equestre Internationale (FEI) had been formed as early as 1921, only after the Second World War did growing interest lead many countries to suggest that rules be prepared which would encourage greater numbers to compete.

From 1946 the sport of show jumping slowly became organised. A number of enthusiasts dedicated themselves to seeing that the sport was open to all. There was much to be done in all directions, beginning with the types of obstacles being jumped.

Prior to 1950 fences were built in an 'open' style, without filling, and were light in construction. Pieces of lath, or slats, were placed along the tops the poles or brush. A knock-down was judged according to which of the horse's feet removed the laths – four faults if brought down by the forelegs, and two faults by the hind-legs. An additional hazard in those days, when judges operated in all weathers from inside the ring, was the calling of a fault if a fence was touched. It is not difficult to see why some changes were

essential and why a re-think was needed about the way the sport was being handled.

Much of the success of show jumping, as far as spectators are concerned, is due to the simplicity of today's rules. People can follow the penalties awarded at a knock-down or refusal at a fence. Most understand why speed at some stage in a competition is the deciding factor. But, as all competitors will know, the national rule books are quite complex in their interpretation of the rules for jumping; there are a number which seldom apply, and others which are seldom used.

The FEI prepare the rules and regulations for international competition, and many countries adopt those rules for common use. In Great Britain the organisation responsible for show jumping, including the establishment and interpretation of the rules under which competitions take place, is the British Show Jumping Association (BSJA).

The type of obstacle to be found in show-jumping arenas, whether indoors or outdoors, will be one of four basic designs or shapes: the upright, the parallel, the pyramid, and the ascending fence.

An upright fence includes those built on a vertical plane – a gate, poles, planks and wall. The parallel is self-explanatory, always having a single pole on the landing side of the jump. A pyramid-type fence is one in the form of a hog's back. Ascending fences are those such as the triple bar, spread oxers, and all types of obstacles built to rise away from the approach side.

These shapes of fences, other than a pyramid, can be introduced into a combination, with the proviso that the maximum distance between fences cannot exceed 12 metres (38 ft 4 ins). Distances outside that measurement will mean the second part becomes an unrelated element and is numbered accordingly. All combination obstacles, whether comprising two or three separate elements, are judged as for one obstacle, though faults and/or disobediences arising at any element or between elements are counted and cumulatively added. If a disobedience occurs between two elements the entire combination must be re-taken.

*(Opposite) Hounds seen parading at a horse show while the fences are being prepared for the following show-jumping competition.*

*(Opposite) Annette Miller on Zephyrus at Hickstead in 1990.*

*(Below) Jumping indoors at the Horse of the Year Show, 1989 – Marie Edgar on Everest Sure Thing.*

(Above) Emma Jane Mac clearing a fence at the All England Jumping Course in Hickstead, Sussex.

(Above) The shapes or types of obstacle found in show jumping, apart from the water jump, are (left to right), the upright or vertical; the ascending fence; the parallel; the hog's back.

(Opposite) Marie Edgar, Junior European individual gold medallist and team gold medallist in 1990, seen here earlier that year jumping outdoors at Windsor on Everest Sure Thing.

The measurement of a jumping course is taken from the start line to the finish and follows the 'track' it is expected a horse will take without the need to cut corners or turn too sharply.

All competitions are timed on a selected speed. A horse or pony should be travelling at so many metres or yards per minute. The Time Allowed is the distance of the track divided by speed set, the Time Limit being twice the Time Allowed. Any competitor, for whatever reason, who exceeds the Time Limit is eliminated; those who exceed

These illustrations show where some of the problems may arise when attempting a double.
(Above) If a horse and rider take off too soon, it is difficult for the related distance between elements to be jumped smoothly without the horse having to put in a short stride.

(Above) Taking off too late, or 'getting underneath' the fence will mean landing far too close to the second element. As when taking off too soon, a rider must ask for a sudden short stride in order to clear the second element, not the easiest of tasks when jumping at speed.

(Above) Being correct at the point of take-off, the two non-jumping strides between elements should present no problems. This illustration shows clearly the need for riders to accurately measure the related distances between elements when walking a course.

(Below and opposite) The related, sometimes erroneously referred to as 'true', distances, which may be set depending on the nature of the two elements forming part of a double.

*Horses: 8 m. (26 ft)    Ponies: 6.86 m. (22 ft 6 ins)*

*Horses : 7.60 m. (25 ft)    Ponies 6.55 m. (21 ft 6 ins)*

*Horses: 7.77 m. (25 ft 6 ins)    Ponies: 6.7 m. (22 ft)*

*Horses: 8 m. (26 ft)    Ponies: 6.86 m. (22 ft 6 ins)*

*Horses: 7.5 m. (24 ft 6 ins)    Ponies: 6.40 m. (21 ft)*

the Time Allowed when jumping in the United Kingdom in competitions staged under Table 'A' are penalised at the rate of one quarter fault for every second or part of a second. In a timed jump-off in certain competitions this penalty can be increased to one fault for every second or part of a second.

The obstacles found in show jumping must all be constructed to be knocked down; no 'fixed' fences are permitted.

The nature of the fences, and the manner in which these are designed and built, is the responsibility of a course builder. Once the ring is ready, usually before competitors are invited to walk the course, the judge of the competition will have checked the fences and the details with the course builder and will then become responsible for the Class.

When designing a course the course builder takes into account the state of the ground, the size of the ring and the materials he has to work with. A good jumping course must be attractive to look at, fun to ride over and sufficiently well thought out to provide an interesting and exciting spectacle for the public. The use of coloured poles and wings, interspersed with plain rustic fences, combined with the use of brush and fillers, help to improve the look of any showground.

Today, the show-jumping season extends for the full twelve months, the outdoor season beginning in the spring and ending at autumn, and the indoor season extending over the winter months.

Apart from the facilities afforded by established showgrounds, most of the countries that participate in show jumping have the use of indoor arenas. These attract international competition in front of large audiences, with television much in evidence. Among the best-known indoor shows are those that take place at Wembley Stadium in London, Madison Square Gardens in New York and in Paris, Frankfurt and Stockholm.

Today, as most competitors know, and a wide public appreciates, there is a vast difference between jumping indoors, in the somewhat confining areas, and jumping outdoors in the wider open spaces. Indoors, the bright lights, the heat and the proximity of the crowds create a daunting challenge for both horse and rider, and the 'going' is not always like that outside. In recent years, however, time, consideration and technical skill has been devoted to producing a synthetic surface to compare favourably with the conditions found in the open.

Now that the show-jumping season extends throughout the year, there is the problem of being in a position to support a 'string' of first-class horses. Sponsorship helps those at the top, but others require more than one animal if they propose to compete, even occasionally, through all seasons.

Many horse shows are held entirely through the generosity and kindness of landowners, even though they may be staged with the support of local riding clubs and other organisations associated with equestrian sport. All shows involve a number of unpaid helpers who devote a considerable amount of time and effort throughout the year to ensure that competitors are catered for in which ever discipline of riding they adopt. But, even with an increasing number of competitors, shows are finding it more difficult to keep going, in spite of local and national sponsorship.

# CHAPTER TWELVE

# Horses in other fields

FOR RIDERS with patience, determination, and the necessary ability, dressage offers many attractions. At the basic level it teaches a horse obedience and balance so that it can also perform other equestrian activities more efficiently. At the more advanced stages dressage becomes an art when riders can use their horses creatively as a means of expression.

High School, or *haute école*, which is very advanced dressage, was all the vogue in the courts of Europe during the Middle Ages, and every successful courtier was expected to ride well and make his horse perform various exotic movements. Music was also introduced and carousels and musical rides were organised as entertainment and to present fresh challenges to a rider's ingenuity and skill.

Similar musical performances are still organised by the Spanish Riding School of Vienna, and the Cadre Noir of Saumur in France. But it is the dressage competitions from

*One of the world's leading exponents of dressage, Swiss rider Christine Stuckelberger on Granat, seen here competing at Goodwood.*

novice to advanced or Olympic levels which have beome so popular.

As with other equestrian sports, the Fédération Equestre Internationale has drawn up a set of objectives and rules which govern these competitions at international level. The Fédération emphasises that dressage should improve the harmonious development of the physique and ability of the horse and make it calm, supple, loose and flexible, while at the same time making it confident, attentive and keen so that the horse achieves perfect understanding with his rider.

In doing so the horse gives the impression of acting of its own accord. Confident and attentive, the horse submits generously to the control of his rider, remaining absolutely straight or bending to the movements of the test.

The Fédération goes on to suggest that 'by virtue of a lively impulsion and the suppleness of his joints, free from the paralysing effects of resistance, the horse obeys willingly and without hesitation'.

International dressage tests are performed in an arena 20 m (22 yds) in width and 60 m (66 yds) in length and bordered by low boards about 304mm (12 ins) high. The surface must be level and is usually of sand or grass. Each rider must perform an official test consisting of a number of sections containing movements and transitions, and each section is marked separately. There are also marks for the rider's position and seat, the correct application of the aids, and the movement, impulsion and submission of the horse.

*(Opposite) A team coming out of the water during the marathon phase at the Royal Windsor Horse Show.*

*(Below) One of the three phases at Carriage Driving Trials is dressage. Here is Alan Bristow's team of greys competing in the Grand Prix at The Royal Windsor Horse Show, 1983.*

Dressage is a sport with a wide range of competitive standards from simple tests for novice riders to advanced tests for the very experienced. The horses are graded according to the points won in affiliated tests, and can progress from novice and elementary to medium and advanced.

# DRIVING

Driving is one of the most popular and fastest-growing equestrian sports, and the appearance of a horse-drawn carriage or vehicle, whether drawn by a single horse or pony, or a pairs team or a four-in-hand, has captured the imagination of many people throughout the world.

Following a meeting in Switzerland in 1969, at which the first set of rules was prepared, the sport became international. Earlier, in 1957, the British Driving Society, one of the first nationally organised bodies, had been founded to 'encourage those interested in the driving of horses, ponies and donkeys'.

During 1972 the Combined Driving Group became one of the disciplines of the British Horse Society, and today a committee has been established to look after Horse Driving Trials. These trials are held under rules laid down by the Fédération Equestre Internationale (FEI), and are open to horses and ponies.

A number of one-day and three-day events are organised in Great Britain, including some International Classes.

Horse Driving Trials follow the pattern set for International and World Championships, with each trial divided into three phases. One of the phases, the Obstacle Competition, is now staged at several major outdoor and indoor shows, and is well-known to television viewers. Other tests, covering dressage and marathon driving, have also been devised for those with varying degrees of skill and ability.

The three phases comprising a Horse Driving Trial are:
*Presentation and Dressage*
This is judged in two sections. The first section is the presentation which assesses the turn-out of the horse, the vehicle and the competitor. Section two is a dressage test

taking place in an arena measuring 100 m (110 yds) × 40 m (44 yds) for teams and tandems, and 60 m (66 yds) × 40 m (44 yds) for singles and pairs. There are four levels of dressage test: the elementary, advanced, alternative advanced and a five-minute test.

*Marathon*

This is a cross-country drive over fields and tracks, avoiding roads as much as possible. The marathon is divided into five sections. The first must be carried out at a trot, the second at a walk, the third at a trot – and in this section competitors must negotiate a series of artificial and natural hazards, including one water obstacle. Section four is carried out at a walk, and the fifth section at a trot.

Breaking pace by one horse in a team may lead to penalties being added by the referee who sits alongside the person driving. Separate judges are placed at each hazard.

*Obstacle Driving*

This is basically a test of the suppleness of the horses following the marathon and the skill of the Whip, the name used to describe the driver. It takes place in an enclosed area, the carriages being driven between carefully measured obstacles within a set time or at speed 'against the clock'.

# POLO

Polo, derived from 'pula', a Tibetan word for the willow root from which polo balls were made, is probably the oldest of all equestrian sports, and may have been played in Persia as long ago as 600 BC. From Iran the sport spread to China, Japan, India and Asia Minor, but it was probably the formation of the Calcutta Polo Club in 1862, which resulted in the popularity of the game spreading to England, the United States of America and South America. Indian and British cavalry officers and tea planters played the game in India, the first match in England taking place between the 9th Lancers and the 10th Hussars in 1871. Shortly afterwards the first English rules were drawn up by the Hurlingham Polo Association. The game is now played on grounds not more than 274 m (300 yds) long and 180 m (200 yds) wide, with goal posts at least 3 m (10 ft) high and 7 m (24 ft) apart. The ball must not be more than 8 cms (3 ins) in diameter and must be between 119 gms and 126 gms in weight (4 to 5 ozs). Polo sticks are made of cane

*(Above) Action during the European Polo Championship final.*

*(Opposite) Urging on a pair of ponies in an obstacle competition during a Horse Show at Wembley in London. The width between the two cones is adjusted to compensate for the width of each carriage, and the slightest knock may topple one or both of the balls seen balanced on top of the cones, causing penalty points to be incurred.*

and may vary in length from between 1.2 m (3 ft 6 ins) and 1.4 m (4 ft 3 ins) according to the requirements of the rider; they must have a cylindrical head 210 mm (8¼ ins) to 242 mm (9½ ins) long. The riders wear protective helmets and knee pads; the ponies have bandages and boots.

A team has four players each of whom has a particular role to play. A match consists of between four and six chukkers, each lasting for seven minutes, although in the Argentine sometimes as many as eight chukkers are played. The word 'chukker' or 'chukka' is derived from the Indian word 'chakkar' meaning a period of continuous play. When fouls occur the timekeeper stops the clock as soon as the umpire's whistle blows, and does not restart it until play resumes. This means that although there are only seven minutes of actual playing time, each chukker can last as long as fifteen minutes – the object being to score goals. After each goal the players change ends.

All polo players are given a handicap ranging from minus 2 goals to plus 10 goals, and those with the higher handicap are considered the better players. In matches played under handicap conditions the total handicap of the four players is added together to give the handicap for the team. The team having the higher aggregate handicap concedes to the other team the difference between the handicaps if eight chukkers are to be played. The figure conceded will vary according to the number of chukkers.

There are usually two mounted umpires, with a referee and a goal judge to control the game.

Most polo ponies are about 15.1 hands in height, but some exceed 16 hands. They have to be extremely agile and manoeuvrable, and have great energy. Speeds of up to 48 kph (30 mph) are reached during a fast game, and a top player may have as many as seven ponies at his disposal, changing them as soon as they begin to tire.

(Above) A carthorse mare and foal being exhibited at the Royal Highland Show.

## SHOWING

It is not possible to succeed in the show ring without paying great attention to detail, and the turnout of horse and rider is of paramount importance.

The children's pony classes are usually divided according to the height of the pony, and the age of the rider. The

(Opposite) 'Showing' is an all-embracing word for a variety of classes, in hand or under saddle. Here a young rider proudly displays the rosettes he has won with his pony, who receives a well-deserved congratulatory pat on the neck.

classes for working hunter ponies are judged on perform-ance over fences as well as conformation.

Riding horses are shown in three main classes, for hunters, hacks, and weight-carrying cobs, although some shows also have classes for riding horses, which are judged more on the way in which they perform in the ring than on their conformation or action.

Whatever the class, the judge will be looking for the best animal, and the rider's task is to show his horse or pony off to the best advantage.

Most of the shows in the United States are held under the jurisdiction of the American Horse Show Association, and their showing classes cater for every type of activity and breed. The classes are usually divided into three styles of riding. The hunting seat is the English style of riding for showing thoroughbreds, the saddle seat is used on the gaited horses, and the stock seat is used for Western riding.

*(Opposite) Mounted police play a valuable part in controlling crowds, as well as providing enjoyment at many horse shows.*

*(Below) Mounted trumpeters led by the drum horse add a touch of pageantry and glamour to a horse show.*

*(Opposite) Riding side-saddle produces an elegance all of its own, with a number of clearly defined rules applying to the rider's dress and presentation.*

*(Below) Four jockeys are seen battling out a finish to this flat race. The 'silks', or colours, they are wearing belong to the owners of the horses and have been registered by them.*

## RODEO RIDING

Rodeos are big business in the United States, and the contests at the best rodeos may include saddle bronc-riding, bareback bronc-riding, bull-riding, steer-wrestling, calf-roping, barrel racing, trick riding, steer-roping, wild-horse races and cutting-horse contests. All but the bull-riding contest are based on the skills used by cowboys working on the big ranches. Chuck-wagon racing was more common fifty years ago, but it still forms part of the Calgary Stampede in Canada.

Following a meeting arranged in a Sydney coffee house in 1944 when the Australian Rough Riders Association was started, rodeos have also become popular in Australia, and many of the competitions are similar to those held in the United States.

## TREKKING

Boer farmers in South Africa used to say the word 'trek' instead of 'miles' to indicate distance, and a journey was referred to as being so many 'treks'. Now trekking on horseback has become very popular in Britain, particularly with riders who may not be very experienced, but who enjoy seeing the countryside from the back of a horse. There are various Trekking Centres around the country where riders can go out daily with a guide; but for more experienced riders there are Riding Holiday Centres where instruction can be given, and the rides take place at a less leisurely pace.

Trail-riding and the Pack Trip are the American versions of trekking, and trail-riding clubs have also become popular in Australia.

# ENDURANCE RIDING

Unlike trekking, endurance riding is for experienced riders with very fit horses, and is becoming an increasingly popular sport all over the world. There is no restriction on the type of horse providing it has the right stamina. Long-distance riding attracts all age groups, and many people who would not perhaps be interested in some of the other highly specialised branches of horsemanship. Events like the Golden Horseshoe Ride in Britain are very carefully controlled, with veterinary surgeons at all the checkpoints, and only those horses that finish each section in good condition are permitted to continue. The ride has to be completed at a specified speed for the award of a golden horseshoe, but there are silver and bronze awards for riders who complete the course in slower times.

# HUNTING

Foxhunting is one of the oldest forms of sport, and despite railways, and more recently motorways which have spoiled large areas of hunting country, the sport continues to thrive with nearly 250 packs of foxhounds in the British Isles, and many others in various parts of the world including more than one hundred in the United States. Hunting is no longer exclusively for the rich and the titled. In addi-

*(Opposite) Calf-roping at a rodeo. Most of the rodeo contests are based on essential cowboy skills.*

*(Below) Trekking across Exmoor in south-west England. This equestrian activity has become very popular with inexperienced riders who just enjoy being on a horse or pony and seeing the countryside. As with all equestrian mounted activities, hard hats should be worn.*

tion, there are many thousands of people who follow hounds either on horseback, on foot or by car and they do so because they thoroughly enjoy the sport and watching hounds at work.

The type of horse required will vary considerably according to the type of country being hunted by a particular pack of hounds. A thoroughbred is an ideal type of horse for the shire packs in Leicestershire, North-

amptonshire and Warwickshire, providing it can jump stout fences, gallop over miles of grassland, and negotiate heavy plough. In the South of England, where the hunting

*(Opposite) A team of heavy working horses taking part in one of the ploughing matches which are still a traditional event in many parts of the British Isles.*

*(Below) Time for a rest during a long distance ride.*

is more enclosed, and there is a considerable amount of woodland, a smaller and more agile type of horse would be better suited to the conditions. Any fit, well-mannered horse or pony can be taken hunting, however, providing it can jump, and its rider is willing to understand any limitations the horse may have as regards speed and stamina.

Hunting in Europe has had to be curtailed due to the threat of rabies, but foxhunting in the United States is still thriving. Hunting in Britain and Ireland is looked upon by experienced hunting enthusiasts as being without equal anywhere in the world.

*(Opposite) Hunting is a traditional sport where people follow different types of hound across country, either mounted or on foot, in pursuit of the fox, the stag or the hare. Many top steeplechasers and event horses have gained valuable experience in the hunting field.*

*(Below) Steeplechasing is one of the most exciting of all forms of horse racing. The first steeplechase is said to have taken place in Ireland in 1752, when riders set their course as the fastest route between one church steeple and another. Racing over properly constructed fences and obstacles was first introduced at Bedford in England in 1810.*

*Harness or trotting racing is growing in popularity. These races are a test of speed, usually over a distance of about one mile. The trotter (the name given to a horse used in harness racing) is drawing a vehicle known as a 'sulky'.*

# Index

# Index

# Illustration acknowledgments

The photographs in this book were supplied by Equestrian Photographic Services, with the exception of the following: All Sport, Morden–Dave Bunce 117; Animal Photography–Sally Anne Thompson 10, 34; Evening Standard 114; Farming Press, Ipswich 28 bottom, 38 top right, 38 bottom right; David Guiver, Wallington 115; *Horse and Hound*, London 120; Kit Houghton, Bridgwater 83, 84, 85, 86, 87, 88, 95, 99, 100, 101, 102, 103, 107, 108, 109, 110, 112, 113, 116, 121; John Mennell, Sherborne 122; H.S. Newsham, Stourport 119; Mike Roberts, Greenford 111, 124; Peter Roberts, London 38 top left, 38 bottom left; Solitaire, Crawley 118; Sport & General Press Agency, London 123.